CHRIST WALKS
WHERE EVIL REIGNED

RESPONDING TO THE RWANDAN GENOCIDE

CHRIST WALKS
WHERE EVIL REIGNED

RESPONDING TO THE RWANDAN GENOCIDE

Emmanuel M. Kolini ARCHBISHOP OF RWANDA
& Peter R. Holmes PhD

Authentic

COLORADO SPRINGS • LONDON • HYDERABAD

Authentic Publishing
We welcome your questions and comments.
USA   1820 Jet Stream Drive, Colorado Springs, CO 80921 www.authenticbooks.com
UK   9 Holdom Avenue, Bletchley, Milton Keynes, Bucks, MK1 1QR
       www.authenticmedia.co.uk
India   Logos Bhavan, Medchal Road, Jeedimetla Village, Secunderabad 500 055, A.P.

Christ Walks Where Evil Reigned
ISBN-13: 978-1-934068-41-0
ISBN-10: 1-934068-41-1
Copyright © 2007 by Emmanuel M. Kolini and Peter R. Holmes

10 09 08 / 6 5 4 3 2 1

Published in 2008 by Authentic
Published in association with the literary agency of Credo Communications LLC,
Grand Rapids, MI 49525.
Library of Congress Cataloging-in-Publication Data

Kolini, Emmanuel M.
   Christ walks where evil reigned : responding to the Rwandan genocide / Emmanuel M. Kolini,
Archbishop of Rwanda and Peter Holmes.
      p. cm.
   Includes bibliographical references.
   ISBN-13: 978-1-934068-41-0
   ISBN-10: 1-934068-41-1
   1. Rwanda--History--Civil War, 1994--War work--Churches. 2. Rwanda--History--Civil War,
1994--Religious aspects. 3. Rwanda--History--Civil War, 1994--Atrocities. 4. Genocide--
Rwanda--Religious aspects. 5. Genocide--Rwanda. 6. Christianity--Rwanda. 7. Christianity-
-Great Lakes Region (Africa) 8. Race relations--Religious aspects--Christianity. 9. Ethnic
relations--Religious aspects--Christianity. I. Holmes, Peter R. II. Title.

   DT450.435.K65 2008
   967.57104'3--dc22
                              2007041663
Cover design: Paul Lewis
Interior design: Angela Lewis
Editorial team: Credo Communications, Jenn Maslyn, Dana Bromley

Printed in the United States of America

In the eternal hope of the finished work of Christ
we commend

Christopher "Eric" Mucyo Kolini
(1970–2002)
Pastor to street kids and to the hungry

and

Jeanette Uwera Kolini
(1971–1974)
Into Your hands we commend her life

Contents

Foreword

Shame was the word that instantly came to my mind when I concluded reading this immensely powerful and disturbing book. A deep shame that should continue to be felt by the nation of Rwanda, the international community, the UN, and, of course, the church.

My wife and I were among the first western visitors to Rwanda following the genocide. Even the careful preparations by my staff could not lessen the horror that awaited us: the wailing of women whose husbands and fathers had been taken away and murdered; the haunted look on the faces of young girls who had been violated or raped; the tiny bones of hundreds of young children in that Roman Catholic church outside Kigali; holding Thacienne, the widow of the Dean of Kigali, a former student, as she wept for her husband. And yes, my shame too. Could I have done more as Archbishop of Canterbury when I had discussed the problems of the Rwandan church with the former Archbishop of Rwanda a year or so earlier?

Writing a social theology of the traumatic events that began on April 6, 1994, and lasted a mere one hundred days is a most difficult task if one wishes to go deeply into the soil of evil. Emmanuel Kolini, Archbishop of Rwanda, and Dr. Holmes are well qualified to do so, and the combination of African and European perspectives enables the reader to stand back from the tragic events and see the long gestation of evil that led to a true "heart of darkness."

What continues to shock me is the way the church conspired in the genocide and the failure of leadership to speak out prophetically and clearly. How could the Anglican Church, so deeply influenced by the East African Revival some decades earlier, fail to see the danger signs and halt the menacing growth of hatred and racism?

Kolini and Holmes do not pull their punches in demonstrating the failure of Christian leaders in the performance of their duties. Yes, I know it is easy for an outsider to condemn, because I and other Europeans and Americans were not there to feel the constricting bonds of fear or to know what might be the consequences of speaking out. Be that as it may, it is the experiences of the most vulnerable that this small book records, and among them the terrible plight of women and children.

Shame. Yes, but with it goes hope. The Christian message is that with genuine repentance comes the strength to build a new future. In my wife's study there is a beautiful print that the Rwandan Minister for Women gave to her when we met Paul Kagame, who was then vice president. The print shows three small children, clearly orphans, tilling the ground with large hoes. The print is saying "Rwanda is building its future once more." But it will only be a secure future if we all learn the lessons of the past. And Christ will reign only when we, his people, deal with evil through the power of his cross. That is why this book deserves to be widely read.

Lord Carey of Clifton
George Carey (Archbishop of Canterbury, 1991–2002)

Foreword

Rwanda is my second home. I love Rwanda and its people, but this country has been the victim of all five evils: spiritual emptiness, corrupt leadership, poverty, disease, and illiteracy. The genocide only made it worse.

This book is not only intended for the church, but it also should appeal to anyone who wants to live in a better world. *Christ Walks Where Evil Reigned* illustrates for us the consequences and impact of sin on a national scale; however it also encourages us to think in new ways so that we can work toward global peace.

Emmanuel Kolini has been a friend for some time now, and for nearly forty years he has dedicated his life to serving people all over Africa and to learning and sharing the lessons from his life experiences. He is an ordinary man whom God has used in an extraordinary way. I am excited to endorse Emmanuel Kolini and Dr. Peter Holmes's joint effort. Both the principles they highlight and the suggestions they make apply way beyond Rwanda.

As you read *Christ Walks Where Evil Reigned*, you will be challenged to speak for those who have no voice. May this book inspire you to have a different perspective on how you use your personal influence as you live out God's purpose for your life!

Pastor Rick Warren
Saddleback Community
California, USA

Acknowledgments

A large number of people have been engaged in giving us material, talking with us, or reading the drafts of this book as it has evolved. Though the final product is entirely our efforts as authors, a great number of people have contributed and deserve thanks.

In Rwanda a number of people have contributed to this book, but special thanks must go to the Kinyarwanda translation team. Also thanks to Dr. James Ndahiro, Pastor Ezra Mpyisi, Bishop Geoffrey M. Rwubusisi, Bishop John K. Rucyahana, Dr. Tito Rutaremara, Dick and Caroline Seed, Father Dr. Bernardin Muzungu, Nicholas Nkurunziza, Dusabe-Mugabe Athanase, the UNICEF and the World Health Organization staffs, and the leadership of AVEGA, a volunteer movement of survivors and dependents.

Also, we wish to commend the leadership and government of Rwanda for their contribution in helping bring back from the dead this beautiful country. But in Rwanda we must also not forget all the staff at the archbishop's office: Speciose, Peninah, Nathan, Gatera, Francis, Adrian and Liz Verwijs, and especially the archbishop's wonderful secretary, Rose.

In the United Kingdom we would like to thank Alphonse Bartson, Lord Carey of Clifton, and Yvonne Cooper, trauma healer and friend to women in Rwanda. Thanks to Dr. Susan Williams for her perceptive sociological comment on the text and its editing. As we acknowledge several times in the text, a huge thank you must also go to Paul Wood for his insightful comments on the Great Lakes Region.

In the United States first thanks must go to our publisher, Mr. Volney James of Paternoster, who went beyond the call of duty in getting the book to print in both English and Kinyarwanda. Also thanks to Pastor Rick Warren for his friendship with Emmanuel Kolini and for his willingness to write a commendation for the book.

Others in the U.S. also need mentioning, especially Dr. Samuel Richardson for his helpful comments and Susan Grayson who very ably helped coordinate much of the detail with us both. Emmanuel would also like to thank some of his friends in the U.S.: Judge Bart Milling, Dr. Tom Yearwood, Dr. Mike Maitre and family, Sonja Hokstra-Foss, and Bishop Gordon Scrutton of West Massachusetts diocese.

Special thanks are due to Bishop Charles Murphy, Chairman, and all members of the Anglican Mission in the Americas, who welcomed the launch of the book at their conference in Dallas, January 2008.

Lastly, substantial thanks are due to our wives. Peter's wife Mary graciously blessed him on numerous trips to Rwanda, subsequently living at the end of an email. Thank you!

I, Emmanuel, wish to thank my children who graciously gave their father away to the church! Also, to my wife Freda Mukakarinda, a remarkable woman who has patiently supported me in my ministry, even though it has taken me away for days, weeks, and even months! She had to love and care for our nine children while also standing with me. Finally, to both of our parents, who continue to love and support us in prayer.

Preface

As a Christian and minister in the church, I feel we need to remind ourselves of the true purpose of the gospel. We are saved, yes, but it is also about change, our transformation, making us real, making us whole. It is our learning what it means to be in God's image—to be Christlike.

We have no excuse. For in the power of the Holy Spirit, we are not defeated human beings. It is the role of the Holy Spirit, as we learn to surrender to Him, to help us all in this process of change. But it is also the role of grace—no, we cannot do it alone—as Paul says, I can do it because Christ gives me strength to change. This avoids anyone saying that they can do it on their own.

What I am saying is that it is by God's grace that we are able to overcome our own dark selves, our circumstances, and all our shortfalls and weaknesses. We can all be healed, made whole. Jesus told us that He was leaving us physically at the Ascension but He would send the Holy Spirit, who is able to help us escape from our circumstances. But such escape is possible only if we surrender and invite Him.

Therefore, it is not that we did not hear about Him or did not receive Him, but that we are still infants. We hear the gospel preached, get excited, but then stop there as the temptations flood in. So we shy away from the Lord. That is how I see Christianity in Rwanda. It is still in its infancy, shying away from the fullness that the Lord offers to us.

I am suggesting that it is the role of the church to acknowledge both our personal and corporate failures. There is no way we should call politicians to account when we ourselves are unwilling to also be held to account. We are guilty of pointing a finger at others while trying to make ourselves look more holy.

So what are the roles of the church and the gospel in what happened in Rwanda? How do we get out of this mess? After admitting the place we are in, that is, after acknowledging our failures, we must then begin to believe there is a way out. There is a Redeemer. We must return to the cross to seek God's help. We must begin by inviting Him to forgive us, to help us to do our own work well. We read in Scripture that Peter was a complete failure, as was David on frequent occasions. When Peter and David were rebuked, they also found their tears. That is probably the image I will most remember about them. After they found their tears and their brokenness, then they could move forward.

The church is meant to be a blessing to the country it resides in. By its prayer and action it should bring blessings to a nation. But for this to happen we must first connect to God by living more in His image. This is our responsibility now, today, not just beginning tomorrow. I would not want people to think I am criticizing the church, for I am part of the church to which we all have a responsibility in. As Rick Warren suggests, the church needs a second reformation. Part of this reformation must be the church's willingness to learn and live the power to both heal and to make whole.

The East African Revival brought God's values to Africa. People were taught by the Lord to be in fellowship, to be accountable to each other in love. In this revival we saw no superiors, no bosses. All were equals. In this equality they had the support of the Lord, and His Spirit reflected the heart of God. His values were being heard and lived. We also must learn again how to live these values.

May Rwanda and the whole of Africa know this love, along with its healing in Christ.

Emmanuel Kolini
Archbishop of Rwanda
Kigali, Rwanda

Preamble

I am sitting on the covered terrace in the guesthouse of St. Stephens Cathedral in Kigali, Rwanda. It is winter in Europe and the warm rainy season here in Central East Africa. I am finalizing this book with Emmanuel Kolini. I have been having regular meetings with His Grace, who either drops in and we sit on the terrace together overlooking the city, or alternately I drop in on him at his office across the road.

This arrangement has gone on for more than a year, including several trips to Rwanda, two one-day meetings at a hotel near Heathrow, one meeting in an airport transit lounge in Amsterdam, and a week in Jacksonville, Florida. For me this has meant around two and a half months in Rwanda and much more time writing and rewriting drafts in my home in England.

Emmanuel is a most remarkable man, both on the global stage as one of the leaders of the Anglican Communion and locally as pastor and bishop of Kigali. He once mentioned to me, "I know the price my family and I have paid—especially in Congo. My diocese was the size of Kenya. I was on the move all the time. It was a new diocese, with only one small Anglican congregation of twenty to twenty-five people when I began. It had ten thousand Anglicans and twenty-two schools when I finished. So I know what compassion fatigue is!"

But Emmanuel now has a global ministry and is the archbishop of numerous Anglican communities way outside the boundaries of the diocese of Kigali, Rwanda. For instance, he is the archbishop for the Anglican Mission to the Americas, as well as the pastor of thousands.

My relationship with Emmanuel began early in 2006 on my first trip to Rwanda with Susan Williams. Susan and I were exploring a persistent challenge made to us by Mary Weeks (now Millard). She told us we should take our teaching to Rwanda where many were still suffering the trauma of the genocide. Sitting in Emmanuel's study within the cathedral grounds, I began sharing with him my own journey over the previous few months as I had prepared myself for the trip. The Lord had been speaking to me about Rwanda, its people, and its need.

My words clearly resonated with him, his face lit up, and we found ourselves of the same mind on a range of key issues. We joked about writing a book together, and before the trip ended I had written the first twelve thousand words from the conversations that Emmanuel, Susan, and I had. This has continued, with the central message of the book becoming clearer as we worked through a number of drafts.

But it also became apparent to us that what was happening in Rwanda was also a problem elsewhere, for instance, in the Great Lakes Region of East Africa, Afghanistan, and Iraq. What we were dreaming for Rwanda could easily be extended to other countries as well, where violence, strife, and pain are also present.

So the ideas are ours together, sometimes voiced in theology, sociology, psychology, or psychotherapy, but all the time seasoned with an African beauty and wisdom, drawing on a long history of storytelling and relational wisdom.

I am not sure what the response to this book will be, but for me it has been one of the most delightful and rewarding projects I have ever undertaken in the Lord. Come join us in our desire to "help heal Rwanda," looking at the needs of the great and stunning continent of

Africa and bringing Christ to all those nations where open wounds still remain unhealed.

Peter R. Holmes
St. Stephens Cathedral
Kigali, Rwanda
March 2007

Introduction

The Purpose of This Book

This book is a case study set in the heart of Central East Africa with lessons for us all, wherever we live in the world. It is about the people of Rwanda, the *Abanyarwanda*. It carries a message that is painful, a message about the darkness of the human condition. But it also carries a message of hope, of transformation, of redemption. It has relevance for all those parts of the world where people are in pain because of the actions of others.

A case study is created when we look closely at an event or situation, seeking to draw valuable lessons from it. In the case of Rwanda this means our being able to relate one way or another with what happened and then respond by letting the lessons change our lives. This learning change should be at both a personal and a relational level and as individuals, churches, local communities, and nations.

Rwanda is one of the smallest countries in Africa, yet it has one of the most serious social problems imaginable. In 1994 over one million people were killed, many by those they knew and trusted. The numbers of those killed are still rising as more bodies continue to be found. In addition several hundred thousand women were raped and an unknown number of children killed. These one hundred days of slaughter in 1994 are unprecedented in Africa's history.

But as this book will illustrate, genocide was not caused by ancient ethnic hate but by a fanatical elite exploiting a vocational distinction to gain power, wealth, and control by the vicious weapon of a taught racial hate.

Today the events are no longer news, but the tragedy and its fallout still remain. A toxic history lies just below the surface and is beginning to take a serious emotional and physical toll on tens of thousands of lives. For instance, victims of the violence now have to live with the guilt of surviving. Also, children who were pulled from under dead bodies in their village have no name and never knew their parents. They still do not know who they are.

In addition, women who contracted HIV/AIDS continue to live, knowing their rapist but are too afraid to seek justice. Others are in daily pain, powerless because they do not know their abusers. They do not know when they might get justice or even where justice is available.

Children have also suffered. Large numbers of those who survived were in their early teens, suddenly found themselves responsible for their younger brothers and sisters—forming child-headed families. Tens of thousands are now beginning to show signs of a range of emotional and physical illnesses never known before in Africa. Clearly this is the legacy and consequence of the most violent episode of Africa's history.

But this book is also a case study of the church in Rwanda. As authors, African and western, we have teamed up to reflect on the role of the church in these terrible events. We are suggesting a range of ways that the church might now respond to the situation. Although set in Rwanda, many of the outcomes that we are proposing need to be extended to all those parts of the world where violence is rife and where compassion is needed to rebuild people's lives. Where there is suffering, one should also be able to find the gospel of Christ bringing healing and wholeness to those in need.

So this book has three purposes. First, it is a book about Rwanda, for the Rwandese people. It is intended to highlight what is now happening in your nation more than a decade after the genocide. We hope to consolidate some ideas about what is needed to "help heal Rwanda."

But this book is also an outreach to the rest of the world, to the victims of violence everywhere who need to know that there is hope in Christ. Christ walks again in Rwanda. He has not forgotten such people. He will also walk again in all those places where He is invited.

Finally, this is a book for the free world with a message for a church that may be too safe and comfortable, a church that may have grown too complacent in its success. We want this book to be an invitation from Christ for you and your faith community to become involved in the needs of the second and third worlds, especially in lands with open wounds like Rwanda. Perhaps you will find here an invitation to become involved, even in communities closer to your home, where violence and tragedy continue to scar lives and landscapes.

The Outline of This Book

People in Rwanda and the surrounding lands felt God became lost, hidden, in the 1994 Rwandan genocide. This is the way people often feel when they have experienced violent abuse. In Rwanda, the land of a thousand hills, God is still small in many people's eyes. Satan and evil[1] are often perceived to be more powerful than God because of the appalling slaughter of the genocide.

---

1. We are very aware that by attributing evil to Satan some would now argue we are stepping outside Scripture into what is called "the new biography," begun by the Early Church Fathers. See H. A. Kelly, *Satan: A Biography* (Cambridge: Cambridge University Press, 2006). For an excellent treatment of the problem of evil from a biblical perspective, see P. Hicks, *The Message of Evil and Suffering* (Nottingham: IVP, 2006).

This book, with Christ, is suggesting a way forward. Although God was not in the carnage of the genocide, we believe He does want to be part of the healing of its wounds. So this is a *book of action* outlining some of what God wants to do in Rwanda now and in all countries and communities like it. We will also be suggesting things that you can do if you so wish.

We believe that Christ is offering Rwanda and the Great Lakes Region of East Africa a blueprint of how people and the nation can find healing and wholeness. We all need to learn how to give to Him our right to justice, our deep pain, and our trauma, as well as how to find a way of diffusing the persistent fear of it happening again.

The book documents step by step some of the key aspects that led to the genocide, so we can all spiritually begin to defuse and reverse these forces. With little modification these same steps can apply to all communities with such deep histories of division and bloodshed. So at a practical level, we will be introducing you to the increasing deep emotional needs in society and to a practical relational way that we can begin to help release Christ's healing.

The book is written for Rwanda, for the Great Lakes Region of Central East Africa, a center of bloodshed, and for the church, working globally in so many arenas of continuing violence around the world where loss and damage to human life tenaciously continues.

The book will be of interest to anyone who is asking questions about the power of evil and to anyone wanting to know how emotionally sick people can find healing. Likewise, if you live in comparative luxury and safety, and if you have the courage, this book will give you a window into a hellish slaughter of human life, probably unknown to you until now, and introduce you to the devastation that still needs your help to resolve.

We would also like this book to be part of Christ's reply to the Rwandan genocide. We are all invited to step into the sickness, pain, and trauma that is Rwanda and to find Christ walking there, waiting for us. Help heal Rwanda.

CHAPTER 1

Introducing Rwanda Today

The Christian church has preached a gospel of salvation to Africa. But today we must learn as a church to bring a gospel of healing and wholeness in Christ to countries like Rwanda and the Great Lakes Region of Africa, along with many other countries and communities, especially in East Africa.

Any case study requires an in-depth understanding of a specific situation. It is in the detail of the history, the people, and the pain that we will discover the message that can be shared elsewhere.[1] So in this book we will introduce you to Rwanda and its people. As we do we must not forget that Rwanda is one of the smallest countries in Africa, though part of a great continent. Also, we must remember that the events in Rwanda over the last fifty years or more are unique, even in the history of Africa.

Some will say that the genocide happened in 1994, and surely the people have recovered by now. The millions in foreign aid, the investment of expertise, and a resilient people getting on with their lives, with a significant emphasis on reconciliation from the government—these must have all helped. All this is true. But we are learning that such deep

---

1. Sociologically one must be cautious about drawing generalizations from case studies. But we believe there are clear themes that resonate with other troubled locations around the world.

scars in the history and culture of a nation like Rwanda are not healed merely by time and investment. It may help us feel more comfortable believing survivors have recovered, and some are, but the overall reality is rather different. Let us look at how things are today.

Rwanda Today: The Personal Devastation of the Genocide

Anyone who was born before 1994 and lived in Rwanda during the genocide is a "genocide survivor." There was no part of the country that was free from the hate and bloodshed. It is estimated that over two million people were made refugees, without discrimination of age or gender. One in four of the Rwandan population were displaced. Meredith also suggests that more people were killed more quickly than at any other time in human history (2005.523). An easy, quick death like drowning or a bullet was an "act of love" by friends and parents.

Hundreds of thousands experienced unimaginable horrors, either directly or indirectly. Writes one woman, "I will never forget the sight of my son pleading with me not to bury him alive . . . he kept trying to come out and was beaten back. And we had to keep covering the pit with earth until . . . there was no movement left" (Meredith 2005.516).

The genocide has particularly affected the lives of young survivors in both practical and emotional ways. The shadow of the genocide remains a tangible and painful part of everyday life. "They have never known love, and cannot therefore, love others in return . . . the morale of survivors is on the decline. Their hearts are much more wounded. They are the living-dead who, rightly, feel that they have been abandoned . . . the older the survivors get, the more they are saddened and troubled by the genocide . . . a growing awareness of what they actually went through."[2] What love they may have since known is too little for

---

2. African Rights, "A Wounded Generation: The Children Who Survived Rwanda's Genocide," (2006, online). Available from <www.africanrights.org> [accessed April 14, 2006]. All the following quotes are from pages 5–20 of this report.

them, while at the time of the events they were totally overwhelmed with the pain and its abuse.

In part, the reason for such oppressive sickness is that the original experience of trauma and its emotional damage has still not been dealt with. Many, including children, have developed emotional disorders. Speaking of her parents, one survivor said ". . . they were tortured before they died. And I'll feel tortured for the rest of my life." Many children were troubled by not being able to save their parents, or bury them.

This, in turn, made it hard for them to return to school and to learning. They were unable to focus, becoming troublemakers or absconders. "I think about my mother and my brothers and my sisters. Even my grandmother who was eighty. Thinking about this almost drives me mad and prevents me from studying" . . . "Now he has left school because he used to shout that everyone was a killer, while the teacher was giving the lesson . . . we tried to calm him down but nothing worked." Such children, young people, and their parents have never been taught how to let go of the pain and its trauma. "I often lose myself and ask why God permitted such a horror." Such thinking can easily lead to despair. From a Christian perspective they ask, "Where my family is there is no suffering. Why did I remain on this cursed earth?"

Such despair is continuing to grow among the survivors: "I will not find happiness as long as I live." Others suffer profound loneliness: "It is difficult to reinvent oneself and to be sociable on one's own." Children, often being the only survivors, became heads of child families: "I ended my schooling in order to dedicate myself to my younger sisters' education." The genocide changed little girls of ten into mothers of younger siblings. Such a thing is inconceivable in the West. Others seek to cope with the pressure differently: "At the age of twelve, Floride tried to commit suicide, together with her eleven year old sister, Josephine. Such sickness builds over the years. Time does not heal."

Among the men, tragically, there are few survivors. So those men who remain find themselves in many communities under real pressure:

"Because many of the survivors in my extended family are women, they ask me to help with this or that urgent matter. And I feel under an obligation to put my studies aside." The men feel an obligation to remain strong for the many who are dependent on them. Yet the terrible betrayal they themselves experienced will often mean that they may prefer to suffer in isolated silence rather than run the further risk of ever trusting others again. However, family demands may make this very difficult.

The one hundred days of genocide were particularly bad for the women. Many were left barely alive and purposely infected with HIV/AIDS. "Girls as young as six were gang raped and kept as sexual slaves, both in Rwanda and in the refugee camps set up in the neighboring countries. . . some of the young girls became pregnant. . . many more have endured illness or caught sexually transmitted diseases, including HIV/AIDS." Devota describes her experience: "Eight of them, they were all boys: I was the only girl. The eight boys raped me . . . sometimes they all raped me. Other times it was just the eldest one."

Such abuse and its emotional pain compounds, worsening over the years, fed by the victim's inability to get justice: "I didn't recognize any of the men who raped me, so I can't bring them to justice." Likewise, Anathalie was "about to get married, but she became sick, and her HIV-positive diagnosis has destroyed her future." She contracted it at age fourteen through multiple rapes from unknown assailants.

The Consequences of the Genocide

Twelve years later the victims of the genocide are easy to see. Many are economically under-privileged, have emotional or physical ill health, and still live with haunting pasts, fears, trauma, and loneliness. Today, those who know they cannot cope often feel in the minority, accused of lying or making up stories for attention. Few will achieve the standards in their education that they would have reached had the genocide not occurred. Careers and family life are unlikely to recover.

Yet schools, colleges, and faith communities often remain the only social network that such victims have.

While trying to survive, and even make some progress in their education or relationships, other problems arise for the victims. Many of the mass graves are close to classrooms or church buildings, which were places of slaughter. Also, some teachers and priests were active participants in the genocide, along with pupils themselves. According to *African Rights,* the continuing comments from teachers close to survivors in schools make it clear that the situation has hardly changed in the twelve years since the genocide. They are suggesting that the general impact of the genocide has not faded in a positive way but has merely gone below ground. It surfaces emotionally when triggered by events like the one hundred days of national mourning held every year or when others begin to relive their own traumatic personal hell.

Perhaps the most tangible legacy of the genocide is the effect it is having on the psychophysiology of the people of Rwanda. We are describing the negative impact of toxic or traumatic emotion on the physical body. Many people are showing signs of diseases traditionally unknown to Africans, like heart disease, cancers, and a range of physical illnesses and immunity problems. For instance, it is said that the Rwandese now have more ulcers than other African societies. In the view of one World Health Organization doctor, this is inevitable. It can only get worse.

What is becoming evident from a great deal of research is that all forms of negative stress are unhealthy, but abuse of the body and assault of the spirit carries terrible consequences when it is not owned, engaged, and let go. For instance, in holding on to trauma the body will experience greater vulnerability to disease, heightened blood pressure, increased emotional instability, and fear of intimacy, to name but a few.

Along with the physical-medical illnesses, the emotional damage of trauma also affects people's ability to learn and to sustain long-term relationships. The consequences for Rwanda in twenty to thirty years time are profoundly disturbing. Likewise, how will latent trauma impact the family and community? Will it feed addictive disorders and alcoholism? How will it be stopped from transmitting down through the generations?[3] Later in this book we will suggest that economically and socially we are all sitting on time bombs in a number of countries where death and events like war leave their carnage. We need to begin to defuse such possibilities as soon as we are able. In Rwanda, over a decade later, and contrary to earlier hopes, the human carnage created by the genocide has worsened, not just faded away as was originally hoped. The implications for the free world are profoundly disturbing.

With its very limited resources, the Rwandan government has been trying very hard to meet these increasing needs. For instance, it has provided school fees for survivors. But at a time when interest is waning toward the events of over a decade ago, the entire Rwandan and international community needs to feel they are able to help. As it was in pre-colonial times here in Rwanda, the child was the responsibility of the whole village. We will note in due course how "extended family" responsibilities have been lost, how cultural values have been stolen. That is where part of the problem lies. We are suggesting that the rebuilding of Rwandan society, and all such areas of the world, is the task of us all.

An Unfinished Task

How could such genocide have happened? How could over one million people be killed in one hundred days? The answer is both simple and complex. Simple in that it did happen, though complex when seeking to understand why. There are no easy answers, and anyone who

---

3. D. Rowland-Klein, "The Transmission of Trauma Across Generations: Identification with Parental Trauma in Children of the Holocaust Survivors," in *Handbook of Stress, Trauma and the Family*, ed. D. R. Catherall (New York: Brunner Routledge, 2004) 117–138.

offers the Rwandese a trite or simplistic response to their trauma only adds to their pain.

It is shocking to discover that some, especially among the moderate Hutu and Tutsi peoples of Rwanda, fear the genocide could return. That it was something unexpected, uncontrollable, explosive, and unable to be explained means the fear of its reoccurrence will continue festering. However, if some of the contributing factors and causes can be identified, then preventative action can be taken to lay a firm foundation for the future. In this book, we seek to identify some of the issues, while also suggesting a way forward for Rwanda and anywhere else where the taking of human life and freedom is still prevalent.

It is not that little has been done; a vast amount has already been achieved. The problem is that there is a great deal still to be done. What is becoming evident over a decade later is that matters are not getting any better for many people in the country. But at a time when the need is increasing, interest is waning. In fact, matters are getting worse: "The tenacity, resilience and morale of the survivors is diminishing."[4]

This is a deep concern to us and something that needs to be more widely known. History is being written in the world news every day; disasters, both natural and man-made, continue to proliferate. Yesterday's news is out of fashion and out of mind. But in ten years time, those parts of the world currently experiencing violence will have accrued a similar complex legacy of repressed trauma and its illnesses. In Rwanda, the real work should just now be beginning, and we all need to help in one way or another.

So while this book highlights some of the broad themes, in talking with people in both the West and Rwanda, it is clear that this question is not just of academic or localized interest. If we can gain a deeper understanding of what happened in Rwanda then it may give us the

---

4. Most of the quotes in this Introduction are from African Rights, "A Wounded Generation: The Children Who Survived Rwanda's Genocide," (2006, online). Available from <www.africanrights.org> [accessed April 14, 2006].

understanding to stop it elsewhere. Other genocides still threaten to happen while some are still going on even now as we write, as in the Darfur region of Sudan. Help heal Rwanda.

PART ONE

Introducing a Genocide

Events never just happen. Human-incited hurt builds over time. It is rarely instant. So violence in our modern world is something that evolves. It has a place, a time, and a range of drivers behind it. On every continent it has its own story.

Therefore the place of violence and abuse should not surprise us. Neither should the consequences surprise us. Every continent and every life is impacted by abuse, and it is not going away. But the consequences of abuse are not merely the events of the abuse. They are much wider in their impact.

Abuse and violence may scar the lives of those that are abused. But we now know there is also a generational legacy. Children will carry some of the stress and trauma of what their parents experienced, even if the children were not present (or perhaps not even born) at the time. Especially damaging for family members are those things that are buried and denied by the parents.

Then there is the impact on both the economy in lost productivity and the damage to the environment because no one has either the energy or the will to care. For instance, the 2006 Israel-Lebanon conflict lasted just a week or two, but the collateral damage will take millions of dollars and years to rebuild.

It is all too easy to just look on the surface, to feel sad, and then to allow yourself to forget what happened. But violence and abuse are not like that. The impact and damage is pernicious, deep, and far-reaching. In using Rwanda as a case study, noting the impact of hatred, abuse, and bloodshed, we intend to go deeper. We will look in more detail at the build-up behind the outbreaks of genocidal violence. We will illustrate how important it is in any such situation to meet the people and to understand the background and history in order to prepare a response.

Most of us are reticent to do this of course. We are bombarded by so many images every day, images of pain and suffering, of death and violence. The frequency creates its own kind of immunity. Our invitation to you is to put aside the broad-brush perspective and instead be willing to engage the detail. Allow yourself to feel involved, just as Christ himself was involved in numerous human tragedies in His day. Likewise, the prophets were involved in the anguish and injustice of their societies. We also can take up God's call to live responsively as salt and light.

CHAPTER 2

The Place of Violence in Our Modern World

The genocide in Rwanda must be put into its context in modern society. Nelson Mandela, writing the Foreword to the World Health Organization's *World Report on Violence and Health*,[1] suggests that the twentieth century will be remembered as a century marked by violence and abuse. He goes on to observe that one of the tragedies of this legacy is the way that it reproduces itself, in that victims learn abuse from victimizers. He believes that our only hope of breaking these cycles in modern society is in our willingness to expose such abuse through the example of the democratic process. "Safety and security don't just happen; they are the result of collective consensus and public investment."

But Mandela, a fellow African, makes another important point. Those who live with violence and its abuse day in and day out begin to assume it is an intrinsic part of the human condition. People not only resign themselves to it, they accept it as normal. To quote an American proverb, "Evil, once tolerated, is soon preferred." Mandela observes that abuse becomes deeply rooted in the social, cultural, and economic

---

1. E. G. Krug, et. al., eds., *World Report on Violence and Health* (Geneva: World Health Organization, 2002).

fabric of human life. Once abuse and violence have become "normal" they are very hard to change. This observation is particularly disturbing in a country like Rwanda, where an explosive genocide has left a whole generation traumatized and some fearing it could happen again.

Defining Genocide

The term *genocide* was coined in 1943 by Raphael Lemkin (1900–1959), a Polish legal scholar. He took the word from the root *genos* (Greek for *family, tribe* or *race*), and *cide* (Latin for *occidere* or *cideo,* to *massacre*). Article 2 ratified by the Convention on the Prevention and Punishment of the Crime of Genocide (CPPCG), defines genocide as "any act committed with intent to destroy, in whole or in part, a national, ethnic, racial or religious group," such as "killing members of the group; causing serious bodily or mental harm to members of the group; deliberately inflicting on the group conditions of life calculated to bring about its physical destruction in whole or in part; imposing measures intended to prevent births within the group; and forcibly transferring children of the group to another group."[2] This happened in Rwanda, where "an entire generation lost their childhood and will be forever scarred by their memories."[3] The horrors they experienced remain with them even today.[4]

Lemkin successfully campaigned to have this definition adopted under international law. It was adopted by the United Nations General Assembly on December 9, 1948, coming into effect on January 12, 1951 (Resolution 260 [III]). It was then adopted by the International

---

2. For a list of some of the main genocides from the 1750s into modern times, see J. Diamond, *Life Energy: Using the Meridians to Unlock the Hidden Power of Your Emotions* (St. Paul, MN: Paragon House, 1985/1990) 284–286.
3. African Rights, "Wounded Generation."
4. African Rights, *Rwanda: Broken Bodies, Torn Spirits. Living with Genocide, Rape, and HIV/AIDS* (2004) 55.

Criminal Court (ICC) and by many countries as part of their national law.[5]

But a debate has continued, because although society now has a definition of genocide, it seems inadequate. For instance, in the case of Rwanda, international confusion, chaos, and reluctance to intervene allowed the genocide to take its full course. No legal mechanism or mandate existed that allowed the international community to intervene once it became known that genocide was taking place. Dallaire[6] documents this reluctance, especially where an internationally recognized government is either initiating or taking an active part in the genocide.[7] Rummel[8] suggests we need a distinction between genocide and democide to help clarify this situation. By *democide* we mean the process whereby a recognized government perpetrates the crime of genocide. Modern examples could be Vladimir Lenin, Mao Zedong, Idi Amin, and Saddam Hussein.[9]

Rather than entering the complex debate surrounding these questions, in outlining the events in Rwanda we will use a more straightforward, abbreviated definition of genocide: "The deliberate extermination of a racial, religious or ethnic group."[10] In taking Rwanda as our case study, we focus on one of the worst human slaughters in human history. But we must first put this tragedy into context.

---

5. Wikipedia, "Genocide," <http://en.wikipedia.org/wiki/Genocide> (accessed).
6. R. Dallaire, *Shake Hands with the Devil: The Failure of Humanity in Rwanda* (London: Arrow Books, 2004).
7. R. J. Rummel, *Death by Government* (Piscataway, N.J.: Transaction Publishers, 1997).
8. Rummel, *Death*.
9. In this book we are not attempting to look at the historic biblical account of what some claim was genocide (Joshua 6).
10. For a helpful edited work on the subject of genocide, see R. Frey, *The Genocidal Temptation: Auschwitz, Hiroshima, Rwanda, and Beyond* (Lanham, Maryland: University Press of America, 2004). For a now classic work outlining the eight stages of how a genocide happens, see G. H. Stanton, *Eight Stages of Genocide* (Washington: Department of State, 1998). This is also available on <http://www.genocidewatch. org/8stages.htm>.

Putting the Rwandan Genocide in Context

Violence exists on a global scale. For instance, violent deaths in Uganda in 2006 averaged 146 a week, three times those of Iraq.[11] Or moving to another continent, under the Maduro regime (2002–2005) in Honduras, some 431 children and young people were killed or executed in 2005 alone,[12] an increase of almost 90 percent from the 10 percent from the previous year. It is an ugly economy of violence where it is cheaper to destroy than build, or to take by force than negotiate. Yet on this basis certain types of violence are accelerating.[13] For instance, there are currently 25 million people internally displaced around the world, and Africa has the most.[14]

Major areas of tension remain around the globe, like in Iraq and the Sudan's western Darfur region, plus the sixty or more wars still going on around the world. But not everyone agrees global violence is still on the increase. For instance, the United Nations claims that global violence since the cold war has declined dramatically, while global terrorism has increased significantly.[15] Violent conflict dropped more than 40 percent by the beginning of the twenty-first century.[16] The twentieth century has been the century of violence, so the twenty-first century could be the age for healing wounds. Many voices are beginning to speak out about how to support this encouraging decline.[17] But

---

11.   K. Pownall, "Uganda's Daily Rate of Violent Death Is Three Times Iraq's, Says Report," *Independent*, London, March 30, 2006.
12.   <http://www.casa-allianz.org.uk/northsouth/CasaWeb.nsf/CasaNews/children>. Should read <http://www.casa-alianza.org.uk/>.
13.   T. Holmes, "The Acceleration of Global Violence," (2005), <http://www.simplyted.blogspot.com/2005/07/acceleration-of-global-violence.html> (accessed February 2, 2007).
14.   <www.fmreview.org/FMRpdfs/FMR20/FMR20gidp.pdf>.
15.   <http://www.star.net/content/view/574/37/>.
16.   <http://www.worldchanging.com/archives/003957.html>.
17.   M. W. Ashford and G. Dauncey, *Enough Blood Shed: 101 Solutions to Violence, Terror and War* (New Society Publishers, 2005).

if we are to encourage an age of healing, we must first define what we mean by this.

Taking Healing Where It Is Most Needed

Unless you believe the future can be better, you are unlikely to take responsibility for changing it. By assuming hope for the future, one guarantees the possibility of permanent positive change. It is very difficult to have such a hope in light of the numbers of displaced peoples, refugees, genocides, and ongoing wars, with all the associated carnage and tragedy. In addition, we need to look closer to home at the long-term consequences of 25 percent of people now living alone or "living-apart-together." Consider too the consequences of one in two children living with only one parent and/or stepparent. Wherever you look, you see the need for healing in people.

Although some are beginning to praise institutions for the turn-around in global violence, the carnage it leaves behind and the impotence of international governments and the church is still a cause for concern. Even some of the basic questions remain unanswered. Is there more racial hatred now than in the past? If so, how do we tackle it? Or is ethnic cleansing a new phenomenon that needs a new range of policies to countermand it?

What is becoming clear is the inadequacy of therapeutic care for trauma victims, especially when trauma includes sustained violence and abuse, loss of home, loss of family, and in many cases torture. In using Rwanda as a case study we are suggesting that the lessons we are learning here are much wider than just for this land of a thousand hills. For the Rwandan genocide involved all three: abuse, torture, and loss of life, home, family, and poverty. Only a holistic approach to the total problem is going to break the cycles of trauma and pain in these people's lives. This is why we believe Rwanda has lessons to teach that will benefit all those who have been or are the victims of abuse and racial violence.

Our reason for thinking this way is simple. It is in the most extreme of examples that one will often see clearly what the core issues really are. Looking at these extreme situations helps clarify what ideas and specific issues need to be addressed first. In identifying these, we are then able to see the same problems when they are more subtly expressed in other local situations, for example, the race issues or similar problems emerging from the uneven distribution of aid after Hurricane Katrina. In seeking to resolve complex issues successfully, one is able to then apply these principles to more routine situations.

So we would like you to join us "help heal Rwanda." We are using this phrase as a symbol of all those places in the world that have experienced violence and atrocities. They all need the healing hands of both a God who loves and a people of compassion. So as you read through this book we would like you to begin to think locally of your own situation: What are the issues we highlight in this extreme case study that could be relevant to your life or circumstances? Please join us on this journey.

Group Discussion Questions

1. We have mentioned a range of damaging social issues. Do any of these exist where you live: racism, segregation, or professional privilege of one group over another?

2. Is racism and ethnic-minority prejudice a problem in your church, group, or region?

3. Do you see any evidence of a "divide and rule" culture around you? Who, if any, are the people groups whose voice is disregarded?

4. How do you feel about the suggestion that the twentieth century was the most violent in human history and that the twenty-first could be the century for healing?

5. How ethnically diverse is the discussion group of which you are a part?

CHAPTER 3

A Brief History of Rwanda

Setting the Landscape

As with any case study, we must be careful to approach the subject of the Rwandan genocide within an historical context. By this we mean we should not consider just the facts of what happened. We first place the facts in the context of what led to the genocide and then set criteria for how we interpret them. For instance, it is naive to suggest that the genocide in Rwanda just flared up. There were numerous contributing factors, including personal, local, national, historic, political, cultural, social, and spiritual aspects to the events, to name but a few. Human nature, as complex as it is, always brings complexity to any situation it encounters.

So, our goal in this book is to identify some of the underlying dynamics that fed into the tragedy of the genocides in the first place, while also questioning what might still be perpetuating, sustaining, and maybe even pushing toward its threat today. If we are unwilling to look at these dynamics, we will never notice how similar or different our own preconceptions and cultural experiences are. Meeting the people in their own context, within their own history, is an essential precursor to loving them.

To do this in a serious way, we must always start with what is inherited, what the landscape looked like, taking the courage to look at it in some depth. Then we can seek to interpret what we identify. Thus, in the next three chapters, we look at different aspects of the history of Rwanda. In this first part, we look at some characteristics of the Rwandese people, then at the background to the genocide, and finally at what actually happened in the 1994 genocide.

Who Are the Hutu and Tutsi Peoples?

Most people who have heard of the Rwandan genocide will comment that it was about a war between two people groups, the Hutu and the Tutsi. Nothing could be further from the truth. It is not that simple.

All the peoples of Rwanda speak the same language, Kinyarwanda; and although the Rwandese are comprised of thirteen clans, they never had dogmatic distinctions regarding their type, class, or hierarchies. They were one indigenous people ruled by kings, the *Mwami*. The tribal chieftains and their families, subject to the king, carried the leadership authority role. Among these peoples we note three ways of describing them: the Tutsi, the Hutu, and the Twa.

The origin of the Tutsi-Hutu distinction is still hotly debated even today. It clearly preceded colonial rule, as recently noted,[1] but these distinctions, prior to Colonialism, were never racial. From the beginning, all Rwandan people shared a common language, culture, and religion. The distinction was merely vocational.

The pastoralists had cows, so they were able to feed their children milk while they were young. This benefited their growth, so the pastoralists were often taller than those who did not own cows. They also had visible wealth through the cattle they owned. Even in Rwanda today the number of cows you own is one of the most visible signs of how wealthy you are. Regardless of which clan they were from, pastoralists

---

1. M. Mamdani, *When Victims Become Killers: Colonialism, Nativism, and the Genocide in Rwanda* (Kampala & Dar es Salaam: Fountain, 2001).

were called Tutsi. The other main group were farmers, working v
hard on the land and feeding mainly on grain. These people were described as Hutu. Once again, Hutu could come from any clan.

This distinction was common across the whole of Africa, not just
in Rwanda. Speaking of the Toro in Eastern Uganda, "the tall Bahima
were the ruling race, the aristocracy, a cattle-herding people. Under
them were the vast majority of people, the farming Bairu" (Anderson
1977.41). Likewise we see the distinction and conflict in Darfur
with the Arab pastoralists and "African" agriculturalist (Meredith
2005:598).

Most of the family of Rwanda's king were Tutsi, while some of
their mothers were Hutu! The ruling chiefs under the king were mixed
Tutsi, Hutu, and Twa. If you increased your wealth—by beginning to
own cows, for instance—then you became Tutsi; but if you lost your
wealth you became Hutu. The distinction was mainly vocational and
wealth-based, not in any way racial. Pastoral and agricultural distinctions exist all around the world, but they have never developed into
genocide like they did in Rwanda.

The third people group was much smaller in both stature and
numbers. They were distinguished physically—because of their very
small stature—rather than by vocation, and they were called the Twa.
The Twa were jungle people and had their own distinct culture and
way of life.

Although widely accepted, these distinctions were not clear-cut.
Both Tutsi and Hutu had sexual relations with the Twa and intermar-
ried with them. Also, when a Tutsi family became poor, without cows,
they started working the land and became Hutu. Similarly, when the
Hutu began to own cows, they became Tutsi.[2] What becomes clear is

---

2. For a detailed account of the origins of the Hutu and Tutsi, see J. Vasina, *Antecedents to Modern Rwanda: The Nyiginya Kingdom* (Madison: University of Wisconsin
Press, 2004) 23 ff. For background to Kinyaga society and the history of Rwanda,
see C. Newbury, *The Cohesion of Oppression: Clientship and Ethnicity in Rwanda
1860–1960* (New York: Columbia University Press, 1988).

that such distinctions were not divisive, just descriptive, and they were never seen as racial, since they were all of the same language and race. Hutu and Tutsi were equals, except in how they made their living. But vocation did dictate wealth, since cattle were a premium wealth creator in the culture. But it was the role of the king, who lived above such distinctions, to emphasize that society was one. He led a complex, integrated hierarchical society, where one of his key jobs was to settle all disputes, thereby resolving conflict.[3]

The Political History

In the late 1800s this long-existing culture began to be influenced by foreigners from the West. Initially, German missionaries had an impact; then in 1899, Germany took Rwanda as one of its colonies, and the king began losing his power. This was the period of the 1st Republic, the time when the king and the people began losing the Rwanda they knew.

As early as the end of the eighteenth century, there is evidence that the German overlords in this part of Africa took a keen interest in distinguishing the appearance of these tribal peoples. Like their own Aryan culture, they sought to define these African mountain people in types or classes, emphasizing the difference between the Hutu, Tutsi, and Twa.

In 1924, the Belgians, delegated by the League of Nations, began ruling the region as the 2nd Republic. They brought with them ethnic attitudes and values already established in the Benelux. Racial distinctions between the Walloon (French speaking) and Flanders (Dutch speaking) peoples were part of the Belgian culture.[4] Similar "racial" distinctions between Tutsi and Hutu were imposed on the Rwandese, building on German colonial attitudes. The Europeans brought a "spir-

---

3. Thank you to Pastor R. Ezra Mpyisi for some of these helpful reminders.
4. P. Roegiere, *La Belgique: Le Roman d'un Pays* (Bruxelles: Gallimard Publishers, 2005) 77.

it of colonialism" with them that was a highly contagious disease, and both church and people were infected by it. We would describe this disease as racism.

Under Belgian rule these "German" distinctions became even more defined in several different ways. Rwandese were given personal ID cards, naming them as either Hutu or Tutsi, based in part on the measurement of their noses and their social status, such as how many cows they owned. More than three cows made you Tutsi, the privileged minority who ruled on behalf of the colonialists.[5] This distinction instilled hate and jealousy that began to fester. It was further fueled by mainly "Christian" education that taught these "ethnic" distinctions in the classroom, even though they did not actually exist.

Under Belgian rule for the next forty years, the Rwandese lived with a divide that had not existed before colonial rule and was reinforced until independence in 1962.[6] For much of the first half of the twentieth century resentment was being encouraged against the ruling, favored, and extreme Tutsi, leading many Tutsi into exile.[7]

In the early 1960s, free elections following independence brought about an inevitable Hutu majority, and power shifted abruptly. The

---

5. Having said this, it is far too simplistic to place all the blame on the Colonial infiltrators from Europe. Much of this change began as early as the time of King Umuryamo Rwabugiri (died 1895). So even in the times of the kings both the lineage and clans were undergoing internal change that began under girding the distinctions. See C. Newbury, *The Cohesion of Oppression: Clientship and Ethnicity in Rwanda 1860–1960*, 11, 95 ff.

6. For a brief history of Rwanda see C. M. Peter and E. Kibalama (eds.), *Civil Society and the Struggle for a Better Rwanda: A Report of the Fact-Finding Mission to Rwanda Organized Under the Auspices of Kituo Cha Katiba* (Kampala: Fountain Publishers, 2006) 16 ff. This book was also published in Kinyarwanda, titled *Sosiyete Sivili n'Urugamba: Rwo Guharanira u Rwanda Rwiza*.

7. It is tempting to talk in terms of percent of Hutu and Tutsi, but because the race distinction was artificial anyway, it is unrealistic to put figures on it. For instance, because many Tutsi were in exile, they were not counted in any census, while many Hutu were actually herdsmen. So we prefer to talk about *extreme* Tutsi or *extreme* Hutu who were leading and feeding this racism, rather than go for a simplistic Hutu-Tutsi distinction.

oppressed Hutu came to power. In 1973 a coup brought General Habyarimana to power. He continued the marginalization and oppression of the Tutsi in a reign lasting for twenty-one years, until his death on April 6, 1994. This assassination sparked the beginning of the 1994 genocide.

As early as 1979, the Tutsi exiled in Kenya had launched the National Rwandan Union. In 1986 this became the Rwandan Patriotic Front (RPF). Its commander, General Fred Rwigyema, was killed early in the struggle, following an invasion in October 1990. So Major Paul Kagame, who had grown up in the same refugee camp as Rwigyema, returned from the U.S. to lead the RPF. Kagame turned the RPF invasion into a fully fledged guerrilla war that they won against the forces of the Habyarimana.

Mamdani suggests that it was the Belgium colonialists who hardened the distinctions between Hutu and Tutsi, with the Hutu as the indigenous Bantu and the Tutsi as alien Hamites.[8] Not everyone agrees, but whatever the outcome of these debates, what is clear is that the tension between the two groups was used for political and economic ends, and it simmers just below the surface even today. For instance, a Tutsi living in the West mentioned he was unwilling to go to the Rwandan congregation in his area, since it was Hutu.

The Rwandese People

Before looking more closely at the background to the genocide, we should note something else about the Rwandese. It becomes obvious to anyone working in Rwanda or who has Rwandese friends that they are not typical Africans. They have little of the flamboyant choleric nature of other African races. Instead, though somewhat embarrassing to admit, they are in some ways close to the English or German temperament. Let us explain what we mean.

---

8. Mamdani, *Victims*.

From an early age a little boy is told to not show his feelings, especially not his tears. Likewise, he is to keep private what he really feels or thinks until it is appropriate, and appropriate times are rare. Prof. Peter Rwanyindo Ruzirabwoba, director of the Institute for Research and Dialogue for Peace (IRDP) in Rwanda, suggests that in Rwandese culture, men showing tears is a sign of weakness; instead, tears need to flow inside. This makes people very private, even secretive and unintentionally deceptive, with their instinct being to say nothing. It would not even occur to them to introduce their name unless invited to do so.

In a culture where "no" is rarely used and challenging your superiors or speaking your mind is frowned upon, creating a culture of open and transparent relationships that facilitate healing is a real challenge! In the current climate people do not trust each other. Prof. Simeon Gasiberege is one of the few psychotherapists in the country. He has had to invest significant time when establishing therapeutic support groups, having to teach them five "protecting rules" he has devised specifically to give group members confidence to begin speaking openly of their experience.

We must stress this personality type is not true of other African peoples. The Great Lakes Region of East Africa proliferates with tribes, language groups, and a diversity of temperaments. But among them all is Rwanda, land of the thousand hills, where a unique African culture and people have grown up that have few of the native personality traits of this part of the world. Instead, in some ways Rwandese would be best at home alongside the stiff upper-lip of the British.

So having looked at the history and temperament of Rwanda, let us now look in more detail at the background to the Genocide.

Group Discussion Questions

1. Were the Rwandese people fairly treated?

2. How similar is the Rwandese temperament to yours?

3. If you inherited responsibility for this region of Africa, how would you rule it?

4. What do you think the Colonial masters did wrong?

5. Were the Rwandese people justly treated?

CHAPTER 4

Drawing the Landscape
Behind the Genocide

The Undermining of a Culture

Rwanda is an interesting case study in what happens when a society that has existed for hundreds of years goes through a shift of authority. We now see the consequences of a way of life suited to a people and owned by them being subversively replaced by a government system that is alien to them. When this new form of governance was imposed on the people, it did not take into account the depth and authority of the way of life already being successfully lived by the people. In retrospect, it suggests to us that monarchy and democracy as we know it in the western world may not be the best governance structure for every society on earth.

By replacing the monarchy as it existed in Rwanda until the end of the eighteenth century, and then undermining the authority and values of traditional Rwandese society, as both the missionaries and then the colonials did, we see a progressive fragmenting of the culture. Those cohesive elements of the culture that held traditional Rwandese society together inevitably began to break down. Things like the traditional justice system, the authority of the king, and the successful balance between pastoralists and farmers were all overturned when first the missionaries and then the colonialists arrived.

Agriculturalist Versus Herdsman

The colonial attitude was that if one could manipulate the ruling group, it would facilitate them as a colonizer. So they used the Tutsi to manage by indirect rule. The colonials made all the decisions but ordered others to implement them. The Belgians gave the orders, but the Tutsi implemented them, getting blamed by the Hutu for what happened.

Inevitably, these distinctions between Hutu and Tutsi fed division and jealousy. There was an inequality in the distribution of power and of resources. In any society where such division occurs, some people become marginalized. During the Colonial period, Tutsi were seen as the "middle class" and Hutu the "working class." What had been merely a distinction between livelihoods became over time racially based hatred that was deeply ingrained in the culture.

The practices of one's livelihood, pastoralist or herdsman, continually reinforced these divisions, though in retrospect it is likely that the area that brought the most long-term damage was the misuse of the education system.

During Belgian rule, most of the education was church-based and colonial in values, promoting Tutsi and humiliating Hutu. For instance, the Belgian colonial government offered financial inducement in the form of subsidies to the Catholic Church and its missionaries,[1] who ran the schools and successfully trained administrators for work in the Colonial government. But for these roles the government de-

---

1. Father Stefaan Minnaert of the Missionnaires d'Afrique explains that from its founding in 1900, the Catholic Church of Rwanda has struggled with ambiguity, by ideology standing with the poor, yet institutionally supporting the ruling powers P. S. M. A. Minneart, *Premier Voyage de Mgr Hirth au Rwanda: Novembre 1899–Février 1900. Contribution à l'étude de la Fondation de l'Eglise Catholique au Rwanda* (Kigali: 2006). (Thank you Lisette Verwijs for this reference).

manded Tutsi. Not all Tutsi benefited, of course. Some were discriminated against in a way similar to the Hutu. But it is clear that the Tutsi were favored, and the Hutu majority were denied access to both education and power.

This favor lasted for a generation. Children born when Belgian rule began were over forty years old when Rwanda was granted independence. Many of these men and women had a lifetime of resentment and bitterness when the Hutus finally came to power. Then there was terrible reverse discrimination in the classroom. Teachers would make Tutsi children stand up and be mocked. They were required to say, "Teacher, forgive me, I will never again be a Tutsi . . ." Even among Tutsi parents, children were named with terms of contempt. For instance, *makaku* means "monkey," while *nomdechien* means "you are a dog." Many Tutsi used these phrases to name their children without fully knowing what the names meant.

Under the Hutu majority in the 1980s, the educational system changed and a concessional policy was introduced. But still only 10 percent of Tutsi were allowed into secondary schools, and even these places were offered to the weak. So they left after a year because they could not handle the demands. Although the government was seen to be implementing greater equality, like the 10 percent of Tutsi as mentioned above, the way it was practiced meant that most Tutsi never graduated.

Where Was the Church?

The church, rather than stand against all of this racism and discrimination, seems to have colluded with it, denying education to most of the children because it was less profitable financially. "The administration wanted a Tutsi bureaucracy, and the church's education program supplied it, thus consolidating the ethnic definitions of an artificial and iniquitous class structure."[2]

Though we generally agree with this comment, it is not entirely true. There are few aspects of Rwanda's history that can be summarized that simplistically. The colonialists favored the chiefs' children, not necessarily all Tutsi children. They targeted the children of those in power. Some of the chiefs were Hutu, and their children were likewise favored. So it is wrong to talk about a Tutsi bureaucracy, because it creates the impression that the rulers were all Tutsi and only Tutsi. They were not. Instead, the rulers were *some* of the children of the chiefs.

What we are suggesting is that a racist church was planted in Rwanda by both the Colonialists and some missionaries. Today, some suggest that this racism is still present in the church. Regardless of which group dominates at any one time, oppression will continue until it is specifically and deliberately exorcized.

In a similar way to the tension in the church, feelings still run very high against the Germans and Belgians for the appalling racist inheritance they left the Rwandese. Comments Paul Wood,

> It is probably not just a coincidence that Belgium was the key colonial player in Rwanda. Itself a blood-soaked land partnering and soaking overseas territories in blood. I'm not saying we should blame the Belgians for the genocide, but there is a bigger picture that may be helpful . . . In the first and second world wars on a massive scale the fathers sacrificed the sons to the national gods. It happened that much of that blood was spilt on Belgian soil . . . a place of sacrifice. Was Rwanda, like Belgium, a primary place of sacrifice in the interplay of

---

2. J. Reader, *Africa: A Biography of the Continent* (London: Penguin, 1998) 629.

powers over-arching a far larger territory? [3]

In Europe the parents gave the children to death, whereas in Rwanda it was the intentional killing of the boys that was intended to bring an end to war.

So when we use the term *racism* in this book we are speaking of something unique to the Rwandan setting. We are not just talking about racism as we know it in the western world—one ethnic group inciting hate against another. In Rwanda it was a learned racism, a hate that was taught in an imaginary ethnic divide in order to justify prejudice against the Tutsi, treating them as foreigners so Hutu were allowed to hate them.

In the 1960s, Tutsi were talked about as if they were dispossessed Jews. This ideology was taught and bred, not just defined by physical features and distinguishing marks of race. It was also a racism bred from the heart, incited and fed by an ideology that was intended to divide and rule. It was the creating of an artificial race that one was taught to hate, even when the race did not actually exist in the way it was claimed. Let us not forget that these were one people, one race, deceived into believing they were different. Paul Wood continues:

> There is an old conflict between agricultural and pastoral which first appears in the account of Cain and Abel (Genesis 4). Some commentators have tried to make a case for one lifestyle being more sacred than another, which I would not support. Others have used the fruits of land and soil as metaphors for spiritual principles, which, though interesting is not compelling for me. But the two lifestyles have often conflicted over issues of land use. I only mention this to suggest that it is somehow connected, perhaps more than coinciden-

---

3. Paul Wood lived and studied in Egypt for a number of years, with a particular interest in the Great Lakes and Nile Regions of Central and North East Africa. He kindly offered to comment on some of our ideas, and these are included throughout the book.

tally, in the first murder recorded in the Bible.[4]

Genesis 4:2 lays the foundation for this suggestion. Abel kept flocks (the herdsman), and Cain worked the soil (the agronomist). Abel brought the firstborn of the flock as an offering (verse 3) to give back to God, while Cain brought some fruit, which displeased God. (Perhaps the fruit that Cain brought was not the first fruits.) Cain then got angry with God (verse 6), and it is interesting to note God's reply, "If you do what is right . . . if not, sin is crouching at your door" (verse 7).

The consequence of Cain's anger was murder (verse 8), and his justification ignored any responsibility to fellow men. "Am I my brother's keeper?" (verse 9). We read that Abel's blood cries out from the ground, for the ground is under a curse (verses 10–11), no longer yielding crops (verse 12). Could this possibly be a partial explanation for the droughts and famines in Africa? Also, one of the outcomes of such sin makes for restless wandering, living under the power and fear of men. Perhaps this was a root of the subsequent slavery (verses 12–14). While God cleansed mankind (Genesis 6:7), the ground remained cursed.[5] One wonders whether such curses still need lifting.

Whatever the roots of this division between agriculturalist and herdsman, the hate festered and grew throughout the colonialist era. Things began to boil over in the late 1950s, eventually leading to the 1959 genocide. Figures differ widely, but between 20,000 and 100,000 people were killed, and some estimates suggest that over 100,000 fled to Burundi, the Congo, Tanzania, and Uganda.

Some Tutsi were also sent into "exile" in their own country to Bugesara. This was a region in southeastern Rwanda infested with tsetse flies and poisonous snakes. Many died while displaced in this region. It was also the area where the invading Tutsi from Burundi entered the

---

4. This is an extract from personal correspondence.
5. Thanks to Patrick Davidson for these thoughts.

country, so the local exiled people suffered a great deal. The region has never been economically developed until now, with the plan to build a dual highway to the new international airport and an international girls school, among other projects.

During the first outbreak of genocide, the church stood against it. Numerous stories are told of missionaries, priests, and Christian leaders standing against the genocidals, siding with the afflicted rather than helping promote the murder, as some of the church did. For both the church and society, these early events should have been a warning of what simmered just below the surface and what could boil over into something much worse. This proved to be the case. So what really happened in the 1994 genocide?

Group Discussion Questions

1. What do you feel about the unhelpful changes brought to traditional Rwandese culture by the foreigners?

2. Do you see any parallels between the Hutu and Tutsi distinction and your own society?

3. Is it right to have such "class" distinctions?

4. Does democracy as we know it lessen or increase such distinctions?

5. What are your feelings about the role of the church in Rwanda?

6. What do you think of the suggestion that the Hutu-Tutsi problem can be found in early Scripture?

7. What would you want to do to change Rwandese society now?

CHAPTER 5

The Genocide:
What Actually Happened?

Who Is Judge and Jury?

By taking the Rwandese situation as a model of what can go wrong in a culture, we are not suggesting that the Rwandese as a people are worse than others. This is not true. When tragedy befalls a society, like the Gulag in the Soviet Union or the killing of the Kurds by the Turks, we are not making a moral judgment of what is right or wrong. Both sides will justify their position, but one argument always sounds convincing until the other position is heard (Proverbs 18:17).

Instead, what we do need to understand is that no one person is righteous, while others are evil. Real life is never that clear-cut. As history has already shown, some of the most "enlightened" cultures of the West can be the worst, for example, the slaughter of the native Indians of North America or the murder of those during the Inquisition. It is important to recognize that such a fate can befall even the best of societies.

But what we also need to note is that socially nothing happens quickly. When a society implodes with racist hate and carnage, it will not have "just happened." It will have built over many years. Most of the significant things that take place in our society happen slowly, gradually. It is not the overnight news that changes society, but rather the gradual mega-trends that happen over time. They often go unnoticed, being gradual changes, which bring about lasting deep change to society or culture, good or bad. Let us now look at how a number of social, racial, political, and economic factors flowed into one another, leading to the worst genocide in African history.

The Events

From the early 1990s onward, militias were being financed and trained to torture and kill both Tutsi and moderate Hutu. Their killing fields were the villages on the fringes of the country. Some have suggested that they were learning this under the skillfull eye of military experts from neighboring Burundi. You can only learn to kill with a machete if you practice, and whole villages of Tutsi were wiped out during this "training" process.

Then in one hundred days, from April to July 1994, it is estimated that fellow Rwandese killed around 1.2 million of their countrymen.[1] The carnage broke out within hours of the assassination of President Habyarimana. Roadblocks were set up, and the killing quickly spread across the country. Men and women, most who had previously been law-abiding, some even professional, took up whatever weapon they could find to kill. Lists had already been prepared of who was to be murdered, so names were read over the radio, giving permission for family members to turn against one another. The violence is almost unbelievable, until you remind yourself of the gas chambers of the holocaust, or the genocide of Stalin's era. Yes, Rwanda's nightmare was extreme, but similar abuses have occurred before and tragically will no doubt occur again.

---

1. These figures are constantly being revised and increased as more mass graves are being found. This figure of 1.2 million is from one of the key survivor agencies, though some estimates still place the figure at around 500,000.

We can estimate that one in eight Rwandese who were in the country at the time were killed. An average of more than 10,000 people were killed every day. It is thought that around 300,000 of these were children. Mass graves are still being found: for instance, another 40,000 bodies were found and properly buried in the Nyamasheke District on April 7, 2006, in the presence of the president of Rwanda and his entire Cabinet.[2] But in addition to those who were killed (often after being tortured), it is also estimated that around 500,000 women were raped. Many of them were intentionally infected with AIDS/HIV. The numbers involved in this range of atrocities are still rising.[3]

Despite the sterling effort at the time of the UN Chief in Rwanda, Major General Roméo Dallaire, it was not the international community that halted this genocide.[4] It was the RPF (Rwandan Patriotic Front), a so-called "rebel" army made up mainly of Tutsi, that intervened by entering Kigali on July 4, 1994. Murekezi[5] has recently noted the fact that Rwanda had to resolve its own problems as the free world played spectator. The genocide was brought to an end by the persecuted

---

2. In this book we will not attempt to document large numbers of stories, just a few for illustrative purposes. This has already been ably done in two volumes by African Rights, *Rwanda: Death, Despair and Defiance* (London: African Rights, 1995). Also, an award-winning popular account is P. Gourevitch, *We Wish to Inform You That Tomorrow We Will Be Killed with Our Families* (New York: Picador, 1998).
3. For a helpful summary of the key events, see <http://newsvote.bbc.co.uk/mpapps/pagetools/print/news.bbc.co.uk/1/hi/world/africa/1288230.stm>. For a more detailed report, see *Leave None to Tell the Story: Genocide in Rwanda* (Human Rights Watch Report, March 1999), also available at <http://www.hrw.org/reports/1999/rwanda/Geno15-8-03.htm#P803_251203>. Also see *The International Commission of Inquiry into Human Rights Abuse in Rwanda* (1999).
4. The absolute failure of the UN/UNAMIR initiative, and the failure of the Arusha Agreement, is well documented in African Rights, *Left to Die: At ETO and Nyanza: The Stories of Rwandese Civilians Abandoned by UN Troops on April 11, 1994* (2001). Also L. R. Melvern, *A People Betrayed: The Role of the West in Rwanda's Genocide* (London: Zed Books, 2000), looks at the failure of the West as a whole.
5. A. A. Murekezi, "Don't Patronize or Belittle Rwandan Christians Committed to Progress," (2006, online), <http://www.christianitytoday.com/ct/2006/004/19.98.html> (accessed April 15, 2006).

themselves. Three remarkable personal accounts of what happened to individuals at this time have recently been published.[6] But let us look at the reality of what happened.

Looking at the Spiritual Landscape of the Genocide

It feels paradoxical to remember that Rwanda was the location of one of the most significant spiritual movements in Africa during the 1900s, the East African Revivals. In the Revivals there was a movement from God emphasizing equality, open confession, and restoration of relationship. We will consider this movement in chapter 6. Perhaps it was God's preparation to the genocides that He saw coming.

But during the 1930s a second spiritual force was at work, a colonial power spiritually undermining the authority of the king by slowly dismantling his traditional spiritual authority. The *bazungu* (foreigners), behind the newly educated nationals, used education to undermine the king and his traditional value systems. The culture was being undermined and lost. But these two spiritual forces, the Revivals and the loss of traditional spiritual authority, were joined by a third.

There was also a dark spiritual movement that began when the colonialists first arrived in Rwanda and became a pernicious evil undermining the entire culture and promoting hatred of one group of people toward another. This built alongside colonial power, expressing itself viciously in 1959 and even more so in the 1994 genocide. This was the fruit of the ongoing subversive undermining of the Tutsi and the king by some of the Hutu and the foreign ruling class. This hate and jealousy was seeded by colonial class attitudes and fertilized by those Rwandese

---

6. I. Llibagiza, *Left to Tell: Discovering God Amidst the Rwandan Holocaust* (Carlsbad, CA: Hay House, 2006); G. Tuhabonye and G. Brozek, *A Genocide Survivors Story of Escape, Faith and Forgiveness* (London: Harper Collins, 2006); B. Bilinda, *With What Remains: A Widow's Quest for Truth in Rwanda.* (London: Hodder and Stoughton, 2006).

nationals who implemented such social subversion. These three contrasting movements formed part of the spiritual landscape of Rwanda.

There is a startling conclusion to be drawn from this landscape. If the hate built up gradually, expressing itself in the 1959 genocide, then our observation, shared by many in the country, is that genocide in Rwanda should be viewed as lasting a full thirty-five years. The one hundred days in 1994 were simply the most horrific expression of it. This long-running genocide spanned as it does over three decades. It took root long before 1959, but surfaced at that time, running its subversive course until its full blossoming in 1994. On this basis, until we are able to dismantle and remove such spiritual and emotional prejudice, fed and exploited by evil, we cannot be sure it will not happen again.

The Serpent

What becomes evident to anyone studying the history surrounding the 1994 genocide is that it was not an explosive, isolated one hundred-day event. Instead, it was part of a darker history in Rwanda going back into the 1800s. The strands of this history are sinister and complex, but they could be likened to a sea serpent weaving in and out of the waves, one minute curling above the surface where you can see it, then plunging below the waterline, hidden but still very present.

The way was inadvertently prepared for the serpent prior to the coming of the European Colonials, with the innocent distinction of pastoralist and farmer. But it was the arrival of the Europeans that made this distinction more dogmatic and sinister, by developing a system of identifying the difference between the herdsman and farmer. Milk made the people taller, and these were the Tutsi. The shorter more stocky muscular farmers were the Hutu. Divide and rule was the colonial strategy, initially implemented by the Catholic White Father Order of missionaries, sent to "soften up" the "natives." This same strategy of divide and rule was then more directly implemented by the government itself to help exploit division among local people.

The preferential treatment of the Tutsi festered into distrust and jealousy, which burst to the surface for the first time in 1959–1963, when 20,000 Tutsi were killed and an exodus began of around 120,000 refugees from Rwanda to the surrounding lands.[7] The serpent then plunged below the waterline again, reappearing on the surface in July 1973 during a *coup d'Etat* led by the military. The serpent quickly plunged again below the surface where it hid and festered for another two decades until the four-year period from 1990 to 1994, when it exploded yet again onto the surface, building to the worst genocide in Rwandan history. Over one million people were killed, and countless tens of thousands were emotionally scarred. And now? The serpent has again plunged below the surface—for the time being.

Comments Paul Wood, "Such water-serpents are often linked to political and ruling powers, in Africa and in other places, with those desiring political power making covenantal relationship with them involving sacrifice. Ezekiel 29:3 and 32:1–3 identifies just such a serpent with Pharaoh, and even more interestingly for Rwanda, it is a Nile serpent."

So what we are suggesting is that even though we talk about 1959 as the first genocide, it is better to say that the genocide began in 1959 and ended (for the time being) in 1994. When one talks about genocide survivors it is not just 1994, but also those who were in exile from the 1950s. Most Tutsi or moderate Hutu would say the genocide started in 1959, and this is the line, as authors, that we are taking in this book. The events of 1994 were just the most recent rising of the serpent above the water line.

---

7. Peter, C. M. and E. Kibalama (eds.), *Civil Society and the Struggle for a Better Rwanda: A Report of the Fact-Finding Mission to Rwanda Organized Under the Auspices of Kituo Cha Katiba* (Kampala: Fountain Publishers, 2006).

Some of the Contributing Factors to the Genocide

It is not difficult to kill another human being when you believe they are less than human. This was the hate fed to the Hutu about their fellow human beings, the Tutsi. But psychologically you cannot believe others are less than human without an accompanying ideology, like fascism or racism. This has to be taught. So even in the (Christian) school system here in Rwanda, Hutu were told they were superior, and Tutsi were required to admit their sub-class status.

This lack of status followed the Tutsi into adult life. The few jobs with any sense of security were available primarily for the Hutu. For instance, only 9 percent of Tutsi were allowed employment in government positions under Habyarimana.[8] Denial fed the racism that was below the surface as the serpent lurked and grew.

Such a culture also created fear and mistrust. The ideology ran so deep that even in families of "mixed" marriages, children could be treated very differently, depending on their appearance. Parents would know that one child was more Tutsi, another more Hutu. It was common for the parent and child who were apparently more Tutsi to be despised by those who looked more Hutu.

Such sinister contempt of even those close to you would feed levels of unrighteous hate that became capable of the unbelievable, the killing of members of one's own family simply based on hate of appearance, but fed by this racist ideology. During the 1994 genocide there are countless examples of husbands or wives killing their own partners, or giving them up to be killed together with one or more of their children, solely because they were Tutsi, or appeared Tutsi. Some pastors and church members behaved in just the same way.

But this racism was also fed by jealousy. People were very jealous of what they had, or more specifically, what others had. They were also very jealous for the success of their own. This legacy continues. Even

---

8. Peter and Kibalama (eds.), *Civil Society*, 37.

47

today within families in Rwanda it is not unusual to see one member being poisoned simply because he is perceived to be more clever than those who are loved more.

Hand in hand with this jealousy was resentment and anger at the success of others. Cows are a very important part of Rwandan society, and they gave status to all those who owned them. But the Tutsi herdsmen were the ones who owned them, not the Hutu farmers. It was a long tradition (still current today) that the marriage dowry be paid in cows. So everyone who wanted a wife would need to go to the Tutsi to buy the cow(s) to negotiate for a wife, after her value has been established. Women today can be worth between three to six cows, valued at around $500 each. In Rwanda this is a huge sum of money. This culture no doubt added to the growth of the serpent.

Poverty has also played its part. Rwanda, though rich, green, and lush, is a very poor country with few natural resources and a very high population for its size. Although not widely talked about, its dense population places great strain on the land and its people. In this, the "law of the jungle" probably adds its own tension in that one person dying, as some argue, allows another to live more easily.[9] During the genocide it was thought by many that killing Tutsi was a shortcut to wealth, because the wealth would be redistributed.

Much of what we are describing was manipulated by official government policy to eliminate Tutsi as part of its ideological policy. Kayibanda, the second president of Rwanda and a hater of Tutsi, was ousted by his successor Habyarimana, though both were among the masterminds of this "final solution." The latter said, "We will kill Tutsi until a Hutu child asks, 'What does a Tutsi look like?'" The vicious intention was that this "race" would be completely wiped out.

---

9. This is not as farfetched as it might sound. "The population is expected to double in the next fifteen to twenty years to an estimated 18 million. This raises serious questions about Rwanda's economic and political stability—there is simply not enough land to sustain such a population," says E. Giradet, *Investing in Peace: Interpeace Annual Report 2005* (Geneva: Interpeace, 2006) 30.

This goal was one of the clearest evidences that what happened in Rwanda was indeed genocide. The dictionary definition of genocide that we have adopted includes the word *deliberate*. The genocide in Rwanda was clearly both deliberately planned and meticulously implemented. The sinister intention is here illustrated. The ideology that fed genocide was already there.

Ignorance also played its part in the genocide. Many ordinary people in Rwandan society believed they would benefit from supporting the genocide. Some thought little about it, while others saw what was happening but refused to challenge it. When someone's life and those of his family were under threat, it was better just to ignore what was going on, and let others deal with it. This is what many did, and it is part of the pain they must now live with.

Added to these social forces was the need for solidarity. It is hard in Rwandan society to step out of line. In a traditional society like this one, the interests of the community are more important than the individual's rights or wishes. Reputation is more important than the risk of making mistakes. So people rarely break rank, especially in the extended family. Such "solidarity" makes it very hard for a person to question the community's or group's actions. When it is generally believed to be "best for everyone," who are you to question?

We must also remember here that it is too simplistic to say that Hutu killed Tutsi. Many Hutu also died during the genocide, some merely because they were in the wrong place at the wrong time. Others challenged the threat and paid with their lives. Others were part of mixed marriages and also paid the price, while others actively defended their Tutsi brothers and sisters, paying the ultimate price. What we are therefore suggesting is that the idea of typical racism being the driving force behind the genocide is far too simplistic. Instead, a complex stream of values and ideas all flowed in together to feed this serpent, enticing it onto the surface once again.

Has the Serpent Gone?

Such a horrific and deeply embedded ideology, expressed in so many different layers of Rwandese society, helped promote the genocide. Those of us outside Rwanda may look on and feel it inconceivable that overnight apparently peaceful, perhaps even professional, people would pick up machetes to kill men and children or rape women. But for a generation that had learned a communal hate through so many subtle means, such a call to arms was merely the next step.

The mass killing stopped in 1994. But how much of the ideology has changed? The government has abolished the "racist" distinctions of Hutu and Tutsi. Their message today is a proactive assertion of reconciliation and shared leadership, Hutu and Tutsi, male and female. Everyone born before 1985, however, will have experienced many years of indoctrination of a way of life that was so deeply divisive. Therefore, to change attitudes and values requires a deep commitment. New values in education are essential.

In a range of ways the ideology is still clearly there. One detects a spirit of discouragement, as well as despair at the poverty. Just to give every child a good meal each day and clean water is still beyond reach. Some talk about a "silent genocide" that is continuing, with some people vanishing and others being poisoned. Even the naming of children, helped by the way the Kinyarwanda language is structured, can be a signal to neighbors that you know something about them. An unhealthy fear still rules many people's lives. Jealousy, anger, and even hate are all very influential. Some people still do not trust even members of their own family.

So although the genocide has stopped, the undercurrents in some ways remain. At various points during the rest of this book we will be noting some of these undercurrents and how we might respond to them. But God was not silent during this first half of the twentieth century as the serpent grew. He was setting His own agenda, which before we go further it would be helpful to note.

Group Discussion Questions

1. What is your reaction to the slaughter of so many people?

2. What do you think of the idea that the genocide was merely an expression of racial hatred building over several decades?

3. Can you imagine a culture built on the value of cows, not cash?

4. What would be some of the problems where a community is more important than the individual?

5. How many contributing factors to the genocide can you find?

6. How have you behaved when peer pressure has compromised your own values?

7. Have you watched either of the movies *Killing Dogs* or *Hotel Rwanda?* How did you react to the movie(s)?

PART TWO

Writing a Social Theology in a Rwandan Setting

We have looked at the history of violence in our case study, how it grew, and some of the apparent factors. We have learned about the ideology that allowed such appalling loss of life to occur. But this is like mapping the outcome of an earthquake without learning about the lives and values of the communities that were devastated. We propose that an approach that merely looks at outcomes is inadequate.

Imagine a people like the Rwandese survivors. Having experienced such terrible tragedy, partly as a consequence of the intervention of the colonial powers in their traditional culture, they are now in need of support from the rest of the world to help them recover from their trauma. Should we support them by offering our own values and ways of life as a replacement for what has been lost of their own? Or should we take the time to learn from them what they lost and then help empower them to recover and develop their own values?

This book is a call to support abused people to discover and develop the best of their own values and traditions, to help them discover who they were created to be rather than to make them in our image!

The 1994 genocide and its build up were symbolic of the appalling devaluing of human life. Human life became worthless, so it could be easily snuffed out. When such an attitude toward human life is adopted, everything about the victims is treated with contempt: their children, history, and culture. None of their values matter anymore. One can delete them from existence. In this way whole communities were destroyed, and their local culture, knowledge, and experience were lost forever. So killing people also becomes cultural annihilation when done on a scale of genocide.

What is also lost is their faith and beliefs. Whether it is a native religion or one of the global religions, it is erased when large numbers of people are killed. Also, with such killing all the social values and history are gone forever. That is why a number of those who were little children at the time of genocide now do not know their family names, times of birth, or who owned what property or cattle. This information was group-held knowledge known to the adult community, so when the adults are killed, the children lose their bearings and identity.

With the loss of the social norms, we also see the loss of the integrity of the whole community. It is no longer a viable, healthy local community when those left are the traumatized, diseased women and their fatherless children. Those left alive, or refugees as they flee, all experience loss of community. All that is meaningful to them has gone: loved ones, the seasons of the fruit trees, the local herbal medicines, the best soil for growing the sugar cane, and the best grasses at differing seasons of the year for grazing. All this community IQ is also lost, as it was with the coffee and tea plantations of Rwanda. When all those who knew how to grow one of the world's most exquisite coffees were killed, then the community and its self-sustainability was devastated.

Other things are also lost. What is behind a lot of racial hate is jealousy, a jealousy against others for their relative wealth or success. In the West, we talk about the rise of "selfism," where the individual's personal needs and wants are more important than the common good or wellbeing of the whole community. Words like respect, honor, *and* dignity *are abandoned, replaced by a new range of values like "me," "my needs," and "what is best for me."*

Behind this shift is a loss of respect for values. Ethics become relative to one's present situation. If you have both opportunity and need then you can abandon what you once believed for this new opportunism. In this sense Rwanda offers an interesting case study because we see a social clash of several value systems: that of the Revival, an ideologically inspired racism, and personal hate and greed. Add to this opportunism and you have abuse and far worse.

Rwanda is still in the midst of this process of coming out of these dark days. It is still going through the process of coming to terms with what has been happening on its soil and in the surrounding regions. Rwanda is still learning what healing is. In this we have the privilege of going on a learning journey with the Rwandese people to recover the best of what was lost and build for the future, letting Christ walk again through the beautiful land of a thousand hills.

CHAPTER 6

Taking a Step Back:
The Rwandan Revival

When God Shares His Heart

One of the most compelling problems with the genocide in Rwanda was the tragic loss of faith in God and the church by many people. We have already noted that in the 1959 genocide there was a clear stand by the church in Rwanda to protect those being persecuted. But in the 1994 genocide this was much less clear. Many of those who assumed the church would protect them found instead that the church turned against them. What was meant to be a safe place, the church building, sometimes became the place of terrible bloodshed. This was one of the key problems that we have now inherited in Rwanda. But another interesting one must also be noted.

Long before the first major genocide in 1959, God had been speaking to the people of Rwanda about what was right and what was wrong with them, both personally and collectively. The East African Revival is a window of God's perspective and values that should have spoken to all of us about how we should think and live as Christians. Instead, it failed to do so for a number of reasons. It was a statement by God of what should be embraced, and had it found wider acceptance, it could have significantly changed the events that were to follow.

When God Intervenes in Society

Christianity first came to Africa in the early chapters of Acts. African's were present at Pentecost (Acts 2:9–10), from Egypt, Libya, and Cyrene. After he was led to Christ by Philip, the Ethiopian eunuch took the gospel into the heart of East Africa (Acts 8:26–38). Also, tradition has it that John Mark went to Egypt, was martyred in Alexandria, but left a young and vigorous church that by A.D. 300 had over eighty bishops. In time, North Africa gave birth to some of the greatest Christian thinkers, including Tertullian, Cyprian, and of course Augustine (Hildebrandt 1981:5).

So in talking about African Christianity we should be thinking from the birth of Christianity, not just from the eighteenth century with the coming of colonial or "Kusoma" (missionary) Christianity (Anderson 1977:118). An important part of the spiritual landscape of Rwanda in recent times was the revival movements of the Holy Spirit from 1933 to the 1950s. This extended period of revival was followed by another smaller movement in Rwanda in the early 1970s. These moves of the Holy Spirit are significant for our understanding of the genocide that was to follow.

Hildebrandt records:

> In 1928 two Ugandan churchmen working at an Anglican mission in Rwanda, Gahini, came under the conviction of the Holy Spirit and their need for full salvation . . . Under the leadership of missionary Dr. Joe Church they found true peace with God . . . but this movement did not last for long . . . then in 1933 a wider, deeper movement began. From Rukiga Kabale the movement spread throughout Rwanda and Uganda, southward to Buhaya and the CMS areas of

Tanzania, north to Sudan, and eastward into Kenya where it became particularly strong.[1]

Let us cite some of the experiences.

A revival team from Uganda and Ruanda visited Katoke. The team included some of the great leaders of the revival: Dr. Joe Church, Canon Barham, Simeoni Nsimbambi, Blasio's older brother, and Erisafti Matovu from Buganda. The Katoke students attended the mission, although they did not take to the message with enthusiasm. Then two prefects confessed they had been pocketing Shs. 1/20 every day when they bought the school meat. Others began to confess and put things right. After a time it became more Pentecostal, with long meetings at night, speaking in tongues, trembling, and great excitement.[2]

Following three years of prayer, a group in southern Maragoli

... used drums, rattles, and iron bars to accompany singing. Hallelujahs punctuated the services. Prophets and ordinary Christians received new hymns in their dreams, and shared these with the rest. Worship began with a time of confession, where every man confessed his sins of the past week ... services included a time of healing, and for testimony about God's work among them.[3]

Another smaller revival began in Rwanda in 1970, located mainly in the Gahini region, through the Scripture Union and Peter

---

1. J. Hildebrandt, *History of the Church in Africa: A Survey* (Achimota, Ghana: African Christian Press, 1981) 233.
2. W. B. Anderson, *The Church in East Africa 1840–1974* (Dodoma: Central Tanganyika Press, 1977) 125.
3. Anderson, *Church*, 120.

Guillebaud. Christians became anointed, sharing with all those around them. Revivals are not that common but have occurred in many parts of the world, except in regions like central Asia and what is now called the 10/40 window. This is the band of Islam that stretches from the west coast of North Africa through the Middle East and into Asia. But when revivals do occur they have a significant impact on those around them.

Some of the most notable are the Welsh revival, the Azusa Street revival of California, and those of South East Asia. In each part of the world that has tasted revival, the Holy Spirit adapts His wishes and acts to the local communities and individuals. The East African revival was no exception. It had a message from God to the people of East Africa, especially Rwanda.

Comments Paul Wood, "One of the key aspects of the Rwandan revival was that of the foot of the cross, the place of sacrifice, being the only place where ethnic, racial, and class divides are reconciled, which was expressed in the Rwandan renewal movement in the saying, 'The ground is level at the foot of the cross.'"[4]

Some of the Revival's Notable Characteristics

The revival was characterized by repentance and sometimes a costly restitution. Central to the movement was the conviction of sin and then public confession of allegiance to Christ, and an emphasis on holiness, forgiveness through the cross, and reconciliation with others. It was a trumpet call from the Lord to the people of God.

It also awakened a hunger to be taught from the Word of God, and more interestingly, a desire to "walk in the light" with one another. By this we mean a desire to be honest about one's feelings and a felt need to live in harmony and love with others, along with a deeper desire for

---

4. J. J. Kritzinger, *The Rwandan Tragedy as a Public Indictment Against Christian Mission* (Missionalia, 2007) 7.

prayer.[5] Reconciliation also included putting things right and "walking in the light" as individuals began for the first time to talk to each other. When being transparent became difficult, the burden was shared and carried among the fellowship.

The revival was characterized by a willingness of people to be open and honest with each other. But these were not Rwandese qualities. We must remember that the Holy Spirit came to Rwanda at a time of deep racial division. Guillebaud records how local people were being impacted by the Holy Spirit:

"They could not live closely together under those circumstances unless they brought into the open things that troubled them, such as a loss of temper, which needed to be repented of quickly. When someone failed to do something and that failure irritated another, it was talked about, the irritation confessed, the forgetfulness explained, and forgiveness sought and received."[6]

In putting things right, there was sometimes an immaturity, especially when believers went to non-believers. This could be a cause of real difficulty. For instance, if a person had an affair with someone's wife, he apologized to the woman, but he would also confess to the husband. This sometimes had disastrous results. Likewise, in public confession, people publicly named others and talked about things that were inappropriate in large gatherings.

But overall the emphasis was good, focused around the cross and an understanding of sin, pain, forgiveness, and reconciliation between sinner and God. Then the focus was toward other fellow human beings, and "being led," which sometimes was taken literally. But the subjectivity about the Holy Spirit's guidance was balanced with a great deal of emphasis on discipline, sometimes to the exclusion of God's grace.

---

5. M. Guillebaud, *Rwanda: The Land God Forgot? Revival, Genocide, and Hope* (Mill Hill, London: Monarch Books, 2002) 60.
6. Guillebaud, *Rwanda*, 62.

Where legalism takes over, self-control is not prepared to acknowledge it as human weakness.

Another feature of the revival was healthy self-control and a healthy release of emotion as the Holy Spirit touched them. While under the influence of the Holy Spirit, people wept for hours, let out deep pain, confessed to fears in their lives, and showed a spontaneous open expression of emotion. Fear of emotionalism was swept away under the waves of the Holy Spirit. People became radiant, full of joy, and filled with a sense of awe at the holiness of God and the power of the work of the cross.[7] The Lord was clearly pointing the way to how Rwanda should live as a nation—together under Him. Sadly, it was not to be.

Overall the Lord was talking to Rwanda about what was to befall them and the qualities they needed to survive and even redeem the loss. This revival emphasized prayer, both corporate and private, and people coming together for prayer and Bible study.

All of this was being experienced in a womb of love, where the Holy Spirit was teaching people that maturity in Christ must lead to love and honor of one another. Learning such love, under the guidance and power of the Holy Spirit, was a life-changing experience.

Also, a number of missionaries and European Christian leaders were involved in Rwanda. Among these was Dr. Joe Church, who later wrote the now seminal work, *Every Man a Bible Student,* still in print some fifty years later.[8] Also some of the leaders of the renewal movement from the 1950s onward in Europe, like Roy Hession, author of *Calvary Road,* had their ideas birthed in the Rwandan East African Revival.[9]

---

7. Guillebaud, *Rwanda,* 69 ff.
8. J. E. Church, *Every Man a Bible Student* (Exeter: Paternoster Press Ltd, 1938/1976).
9. R. Hession, *Calvary Road* (Alresford, Hants: CLC, 1950/1988) 8 ff.

The Place of Women

But the revival was accompanied by another significant feature, the emancipation of women. This is most important since the genocide took the greatest toll on women, children, and the elderly who remained. Long before the genocide, the Lord was emphasizing the values of the Kingdom of Heaven:

Many high-class Tutsi (women) were not allowed to be seen outside their *rugo* (the enclosure around their houses). When they insisted in joining fellowship meetings and going to church, it was misunderstood and led to much persecution. Even now, men are always given chairs, while the women sit on mats, and at a recent convention to commemorate the revival in Gahini, I was horrified to find that not a single woman was allowed to speak. During the revival days it was impossible to muzzle the women. Once they had experienced acceptance in Christ, they wanted to tell everyone what He meant to them. They joined teams going to other villages to tell of what God had done for them.[10]

As well as the emancipation of women, the revival meant that the children were given greater status. In traditional Kinyarwanda society each age group had its place. The young were protected, the women had their place, while the elderly, the "library of experience," were honored. In many ways, the revival both supported and challenged these beliefs and values.

The Lord emphasized through this revival a mutual honor of women by the men that could have led the way for future helpful and liberating attitudes to women. Instead, during the genocide, along with the suffering of children and the elderly, women became a special target of rape, though they were allowed to live. The adoration and honor of

---

10. Guillebaud, *Rwanda*, 60. The Minister for Unity and Reconciliation, who is a woman, spoke at this conference and said that this quoted statement was inaccurate.

women by the Lord in the revival, bestowing His Holy Spirit on them in equal anointing, was to be stolen and reversed in the forthcoming genocide. One wonders whether even the western church has learned these lessons: that it is vulnerable when it compromises such values as its high view of all human worth.

The Response of the Church

Denominationally Rwanda was largely Catholic, but the revival broke out among the Anglicans and the free churches. Confessing publicly was strange to the Catholics. Also, since the Protestant congregations were already marginalized, it meant the revival actually gave these people more dignity and affirmation. In addition, the revival was mainly lay-led, so it never had the dignity or status of being "official" church. This was no doubt one of the points that the Lord was making to the wider faith community.

Looking back on these events, it is tragic that more people in the wider church in Rwanda did not come under the teaching and mutual love of the revival. One of the reasons for this resistance may have been some of the foreign Christian workers' scepticism and doubt regarding the efficacy of the revival. Some clearly disliked certain features:

> (Some missionaries) were very disapproving of the excesses they had seen. They considered that some of those affected were verging on heresy . . . they attended a 4 a.m. prayer meeting which they did not enjoy. They felt, and showed, that it was too emotional and loud, and was probably just the way ignorant Africans could express their feelings.[11]

One wonders to what extend such attitudes contributed to the waning of the revival, for love is finding the worth of a person while overlooking their faults (Romans 5:8).

---

11. Guillebaud, *Rwanda*, 85, 102.

One of the other difficulties of the revival was that it was very localized in the Kigeme region, where many people now have Christian names. The revival had a positive cleansing affect. In contrast, in other parts of the country the depth of the pain in the culture is seen in the children's names—*Ntuyenabo*, "I dwell among enemies," and *Ntamabyariro*, "no place to bear children." Given the controlling and private nature of the Rwandese people, it is not surprising the Lord needed to demonstrate how people could live with Him in freedom, relationally and emotionally healthy.

It is likely that the revival helped the church to stand against the 1959 genocide. Had it spread among more people in Rwanda, it would surely have helped defuse the hate being fed into the people's lives by the dominant ideology in the country. Alas, defusing this growing hatred was not to happen, and the church is now perceived to have collaborated with the policy of genocide rather than standing against it in 1994. Nonetheless, before the 1994 genocidal atrocities occurred, God clearly showed people the way they could live harmoniously together under His Lordship.[12]

In Summary

Following the 1959 genocide, a number of church leaders, both missionaries and Rwandese, left Rwanda. This deeply impacted the church. It also ended the revival, since most of its leadership was lost. Those who remained were cut off from East Africa, because a number of the refugees went into Uganda. Before this, travel and communication was easier, but when refugees entered Uganda, the Rwandese who had stayed could not go there. This was further complicated by political problems between Belgians and English, meaning the borders could not be crossed. So Uganda became isolated, as did Burundi, and the revival was compromised. Individuals and small groups continued

---

12. Another anticipation of the coming atrocities were the prophecies of Kibeho in the 1980s.

to carry it, but there was a sense in which it never fulfilled its full potential or purpose. This was also the case with the more localized revival of the 1970s.

The remarkable zeal of the Victorian missionary movement in Europe and North America sought to reach the world so Christ could return (Matthew 28:18; Revelation 7:9). This movement, along with the shattered dreams, was broken by the Great War (1914–1918) in Europe. Two of the world's leading missionary sending countries, Britain and Germany, inexplicably found themselves in not one, but two wars with each other. The slaughter of millions of people led to the subsequent decimation of the church, bringing to an end any hope that Europe and North America could lead the way for the fulfilment of the Great Commission and the return of Christ (Mark 16:15–18). The part of God's plan to fulfill His Commission through the Rwanda revivals was likewise halted through a variety of events, not the least of which were the genocides of 1959 and 1994.

Comments Paul Wood, "I would intuitively see the revival as critical to the whole process because it probably had the potential to not only prevent the genocide, but to heal ancient wounds and launch the region into its calling—if it had fulfilled its heavenly mandate. It raised the stakes over the destiny of the region . . . a detailed study of the revival would, I feel, be very helpful."

Group Discussion Questions

1. Do you see a devaluing of human life in modern society?

2. Would you welcome a revival if it had values like the Rwandan one?

3. Which aspects of the revival would you have found most difficult?

4. What are your feelings regarding the mixed response of the missionaries?

5. How do you feel about the Holy Spirit's response to the gender issue in the revival?

CHAPTER 7

Traditional Rwandan Values

When a Society Goes Through Change

When doing any ethnographic research on a culture, it is very important not to lose one's perspective. It is all too easy to romanticize how wonderful a society is or is not. For instance, when we look at biblical Hebrew society it is easy to see it in a rose-tinted way. Likewise, when looking at Rwandan society, it is tempting to say that the king and his people lived a harmonious existence for hundreds of years prior to the missionaries and colonialists arriving. These *bazungas* (foreigners) then "messed it all up." Unfortunately, most of life is not about such simple black and white ideas; it is mostly shades of gray. Human nature being what it is, we all have a tendency to fall below our own morals in our actual behavior.

The dramatic change in the way Rwandese society was ruled after colonialism is an interesting study. In retrospect, it is now clear to see that under the king and his chieftains, up until the late 1800s, society was held together in a successful way, with pastoralist and herdsman working with one another. It was as colonialism undermined these traditional structures that much of this cohesion was lost. Let us see if we can identify some of these values that held Rwandese society together, and what was to happen when it came under threat.

Traditional Rwandan Society and Its Values[1]

At the time of the kings of Rwanda, until the end of the nineteenth century, society was ruled by a system of courts called *Gusasinzobe.* When a family or community matter needed to be tested or resolved, members of the same clan would sit around the skin of an *inzobe,* an antelope, with their feet touching it. They would commit to each other to be open, honest, and confidential, then they discussed the matter more fully. There was no punishment of those involved if they spoke honestly and did not repeat their mistakes.

The decisions made in the *Gusasinzobe* were final. Anyone later found guilty of lying was no longer a true Rwandan, no longer *Impfura.* For to be called Rwandan during those times was a sign of respect, integrity, and stature, not merely a term for a person living in a certain region of East Africa. To be Rwandan was to be a graduate of life and to have achieved integrity. Rwandan was an ideology, not a geography.

It was an open society where everyone was responsible for the community. No one actually owned anything; property was owned by everyone. To actively participate in society, such as having your children marry, you first had to be in good standing in the community. For instance, a man known to beat women was no longer allowed to sit with the men. The ultimate disgrace was to be sent away from the community, with no hope of marriage, or to have no one attend your burial.

Communities worked together, and the justice system would go as wide as was necessary to ensure justice. A person could be heavily punished for refusing communal responsibility and allowing a neighbor to go hungry. Although the nation had thirteen clans, it had both a common language and a system of justice and was able to adapt to any situation. Integration characterized this society.

---

1. Thank you to Dr. James Ndahiro for a delightful conversation in which he shared some of these ideas.

Allegiance to the Clan, Village, or Family?

Reader suggests that there is a strong authoritarian tradition in Rwandese culture and an equally strong acceptance of group identity.[2] Comments Paul Wood,

> In most African ethnic groups at birth or soon afterward there is a reinforcing of allegiance through "traditional" ritual dedications. It is often accompanied by ritual sacrifice, which indicates its covenant nature . . . its effect is to bind an individual more strongly to any spiritual power incorporated in the group identity. Thereafter, to subsequently act on their behalf, and in its interests. If the church is not already taking a stand on transference of covenantal allegiance to Christ, then this is, perhaps, an issue that will help the church become part of the answer and not part of the problem. Especially in times of crisis these corporate spirits get very stirred up. Africa now has a mixture of both.

Although we accept Reader's observation that there was a strong authoritarian tradition, we should also note that it raises the question of allegiance in Rwanda today. It wasn't necessarily because of the way family values were dismantled within traditional cultural commitments to families and other groups, but what its undoing had unleashed in racism, conflict, and the genocide. Many have clearly thrown these values aside, with its authoritarian traditions, because they have not understood their importance.

What we are suggesting is that blood covenants, or setting vows through the shedding of blood, are behind the living history of the whole of Africa. This links spiritual reality with past, present, and future material reality. Although as Christians we accept that the highest authority is the shed blood of Christ, many other claims also ap-

---

2. Reader, *Africa*, 671.

ply to us. The church still has much work to do in disentangling these claims.

One outcome is that in Rwanda today we now have a problem with authority. Traditional family authority rests with the eldest male—the "gray hair." He is the "Elder." Age gives a person authority. So when a male authority figure passes away, his wife automatically has authority, unless he has appointed one of his children or grandchildren to assume authority. In this case the mother becomes a helper, and when there is a disagreement, the son or grandson will make decisions. With these structures no longer in place, the situation either becomes more fluid or there are no structures at all that replace it.

In traditional Rwandese society the older people carried the authority, but much of this respect has been lost. Both the church and the government have been taking away authority from the home, which has contributed to the breakdown of family life. Before the arrival of a Christian witness in Rwanda, fathers maintained a "priestly" authority, having the power of blessing, cursing, and protecting. The "priesthood" at home is missing now. People are accepting it less and less.

We are not suggesting a return to this patriarchy, but we need to acknowledge its loss and the lack of accountability of people as a result. We are also not suggesting that adults should claim authority unless they are already doing the job of an Elder—a father or a mother as spiritual leader. Exercising such authority should be a gift that is used honorably. Where allegiance to the clan, to the family, or even to Christ no longer exists, people become accountable only to themselves. The results, as the history of genocide demonstrates, can be disastrous. Much is lost, including spiritual values.

Traditional Rwandan Spirituality

In traditional pre-Christian Rwandan society, spirituality was an important value. The king worked with wise authorities, diviners, and God—four distinct spiritual powers. The king was the political head,

[handwritten margin note: How then should one mix... bring the... God?]

with his people subject to him. In addition there were wise people with whom the king would consult on difficult matters. Then the diviners would be consulted on the conclusion of the wise people. These diviners in turn would then go for the blessing of the spirits, for the king was appointed by God, the fourth power, not chosen by the people.

The king represented both political and spiritual power. Both were vested in him. But the spiritual advisers had the final say. If the people went against those in spiritual authority, misfortune and punishment could befall both the people involved in the transgression and the country. So the diviners had enormous power.

Rwandan traditional spirituality had a "father God," *Imana Rurema,* a son *Rurema*, often described as *Ryangombe,* and a mother, *Babinoa.* They lived in the jungles and the forests. Part of traditional Rwandan religion tells a beautiful story about how God spends the day traveling across Africa, but he always came home to sleep in Rwanda—Rwanda was God's home. The title of this book echoes this tradition.

One of the bishops of Rwanda said that in the early stages of missionary efforts the Rwandese found it easy to adopt Christian ideas into their spirituality. They could believe God loved them and that He had sent His Son, that He was both Creator and Father. But it was when the missionaries forced them to choose that they then felt they were being asked to abandon their own heritage for colonialist values. The country was held together by the king and those wise people and diviners with whom he consulted. A spiritual Christ and the Bible, which replaced the king and his consultants, did not hold society together in the same way. Because of this, traditional Rwandese spirituality and its emphasis on mutuality has been largely lost, as has much of the coherence of the culture. The duty to be part of the wider community no longer forms part of the people's consciousness in the way it once did.

For the Rwandese, nothing was secular. Everything was sacred. There was always a connection with God through everything. God was involved in everything. Before they sowed seed, they went to their father and mother (the "gray hairs") who blessed the seed. Also, they refrained from eating the first fruits, because these were to go to the ones who blessed them.

Even animals, when they entered a home or village, were protected. When an animal was being hunted, it could enter a home as a safe haven. The hunters were not allowed to drive it out, because anybody or anything seeking refuge had a right to safety in the village, even animals. Likewise, when a stranger entered the village he was an honored guest. Traditional Rwandese culture honored the stranger, and even the animals.

Confusion followed the arrival of Christianity, when people were told that all they had learned and believed was wrong and must be forgotten. Although as Christians we must not teach what is contrary to the Bible, we believe that some of the traditional Rwandan values were biblical. It would be very fruitful to research and recover some of the positive values of traditional Rwandan spirituality, thereby beginning to build a contemporary Rwandese Christian spirituality. The thirty-year genocide saw many of these traditional values largely lost, by both the death of so many and the loss of value for all human life that such a genocide creates. Perhaps the most devastating loss was the value and importance of children.

The Importance of Children

The Rwandans talk about the way of snakes with sleeping babies. When a snake finds a baby sleeping, it places its tail into the child's mouth. If the baby has no teeth, then the snake will not bite the baby, for the snake will kill only an enemy, and only those who have teeth can be its enemies.

During war in Rwanda, women and children were more likely not to be killed but to be taken away instead. If a person killed a woman or child, the act stirred such a lasting hatred toward the perpetrator that no one would forgive him. Babies especially are innocent; they even smile at an enemy. In fact, a baby does not even know who an enemy is. Babies have no enemies. They are called "angels" in Kinyarwanda

Along similar lines every villager was considered an extended family member. Whoever was around the village took care of the children, so they never starved or had problems. This is one of the reasons why villagers would never tell an orphan he was an orphan. A child was everybody's responsibility. But treatment was expected to be equal, without favoritism, otherwise the child would turn against those in authority. Genocide turned all these values upside down.

One really awful example of how badly things have changed is the justifying of sexual abuse against children. Many years ago a witch doctor suggested that raping children prevents and provides a cure for HIV. In the genocide, it was then used forcefully as a justification for abuse. Even today, it is still used as a way to justify and excuse severe sexual abuse against young girls. In response, the president of Rwanda has asked the police to work very closely with doctors. Even the wife of the president, seeking to restore traditional Rwandan values, has emphasized that one should "look at every child as your own." Such loss is the loss of the value of human life.

Group Discussion Questions

1. Can you see any modern society being run as a kingdom like the Rwandese?

2. If you were an eighteenth century missionary, what would you do differently in bringing the gospel to the Rwandese?

3. Should western society value the elderly more?

4. Do we have "group identity" in society today?

5. Do you see a loss of authority in society of the "elder" or "priest"?

CHAPTER 8

When the Value of Human Life Is Rejected

In the late 1800s, the missionaries came first, then the Germans, disarming the king and his people. The Rwandese describe it as *kiriziya yakuye kirazira,* when "the church replaced the values of the Rwandese." This imperialist Christianity, imposed from the West, stifled innovation and insisted on western court values, implying the "primitive" values of the kings were inadequate because they were not "Christian." Sadly this represented a fundamental misunderstanding of Rwandese justice. The king frequently said "Never!" imposing absolute rule where necessary. It was when the church told people to read the Book and follow its rules that justice became relative and instability increased for many.

The westerners intended to "civilize" the "savages." These pagan peoples were to receive new values from the church, so the king, the chiefs, and the elders were no longer needed. By taking their absolute rule away, westerners stole from the culture the unifying power and authority that could say "No!" From that time, despite the protests of king and people, the culture no longer had the constraint of the king and his chiefs. There was no longer a ruler whose duty it was to hold things together and bring people to account.

So in reality the Colonial masters had a strategy of "divide and rule." It was a breakdown of traditional Rwandan society. A Rwandan joke comments on how bad things were: God called two Rwandese and said to one of them, "Ask me what you would like, and I will give your neighbor a double portion." The Rwandese replied, "Remove my one eye."

God's View of the Worth of Human Life

For people to hurt other people, it is necessary to have a view of human personhood that values others as worth little or nothing. A modern example of the de-valuing of human life was the collectivist philosophy of Stalin. Here the individual was dispensable for the greater good of the movement and the nation. The many were more important than the one. As one follows a wider political or social agenda, an individual's life can be worth less. But before we begin to look at some of the reasons, from a Christian perspective, why life can be worth so little in genocide, we need to understand how Scripture sees human life normally.

"Then God said, 'Let us make man in our image, in our likeness, and let them rule over the fish of the sea and the birds of the air'" (Genesis 1:26). Likewise, "The LORD God formed man from the dust of the ground and breathed in his nostrils the breath of life" (Genesis 2:7). What these verses suggest is that the creation of man and woman had a special place in the creation of all things. God placed His breath in the dust of humanity, giving human beings a unique, supernatural nature. We are a unity of body and spirit; they commingle with one another, giving us our full unique human nature.[1]

We now equate this spiritual aspect of our nature with the human spirit. We share a spiritual nature with God Himself. In one sense, our

---

1. P. R. Holmes, *Becoming More Human: Exploring the Interface of Spirituality, Discipleship and Therapeutic Faith Community* (Bletchley, Milton Keynes: Paternoster, 2005) 75 ff.

spirit is like the Holy Spirit. Therefore, there is something divine and significant in man and woman as together they reflect the image of God—*imago Dei*. Human beings, unlike any other created beings in the universe, combine the mortality of a physical body with the everlasting supernatural human spirit. Human beings are first spirit, an idea in the mind of God, which is then spiritually animated and embodied. Through this process human beings carry the hallmark and the values of divine nature.

So the value of human life is not just in its unique personhood, or individuality; it is also that every human being carries a personal imprint of the divine, so raising their worth to a unique level. This uniqueness of human individuality was lifted to an even higher level when Christ took on human form and became like one of us. He considered human form worthy of divine indwelling.

He also took this humanity back into divinity as He rose from the grave and ascended with a spiritual resurrection body that now presides at the right hand of God (Colossians 3:1). What God had created, He then exalted. God lived as divinity in human physical reality. Such is God's pleasure in and value of human beings. The status of man and woman is both profoundly significant and disturbingly fragile, especially when human nature falls below its divine heritage and calling.

Scripture reflects this value with the Old Testament injunction to love one's neighbor as oneself (Leviticus 19:18). This is reemphasized in the New Testament (Matthew 19:19; 22:39; Romans 13:9; Galatians 5:14; James 2:8).[2] Human life, once given, must be lived relationally with mutual honor and love.

This value on all human life is a challenge to every one of us. Who are the people we treat as less significant? Whose values do we regard as less important than our own? In Rwandese society, it was first the

---

2. I. Henderson, "Self-Love," in *The Westminster Dictionary of Christian Ethics*, eds. J. F. Childress and J. MacQuarrie (Philadelphia: Westminster Press, 1986) 571.

...u, then the Tutsi, who were victims of this denigration. God's view of human personhood is very different.

Losing the Value of Human Life

People's destruction of human life can take place only where there is a devalued attitude toward human personhood, where human life is no longer esteemed. Only when we consider others less than human, "second class," or "savages," are we able to destroy them with impunity. On the other hand, if we hold a "high" view of people, seeing in them the very image of God, then we view others as sacred, highly valued beings.[3] As Christians this should be our view of both others and ourselves. But where such a view does not hold, where human beings are not valued—because of racism or prejudice, for instance—it is within the power of our dark and damaged human nature to destroy all that we do not value.

All human beings have the power to write a significant positive history, with themselves, others, and God. All of us are created and able to write an enduring history. Killing a human being prematurely brings all of this potential to an end. Writing human history is clearly very important to God, since it sees the fulfilment of His covenant promise to provide for all humanity. Also, the journey writing this history sees Christ formed in us. Long life is the fruit and the testimony to God's fulfilling this covenant with men and women (Genesis 17:4; Exodus 2:24; Daniel 9:4).

Destroying lives at any time in their unfolding and history snuffs them out and erases their potential from the earth. The future is stolen. They are no longer able to fulfill their true potential as human beings the way God had intended. They prematurely cease writing a history

---

3. The impact of social Darwinism has been enormous, allowing us to select who should live and who should die. D. P. O'Mathuna, "Human Dignity in the Nazi Era: Implications for Contemporary Bioethics," (2006, online), <http://www.biomedcentral.com/1472-6939/7/2> (accessed December 18, 2006).

with themselves, others, and God. Untimely death in any form also brings to an end all the gifting and anointing that the individual had carried. All of this potential from God should be fully enjoyed, shared, and given in fulfilment of a faithful human life. Spiritually speaking, all gifting and its anointing are given by the Father to the Son as a gift. The Son gives it to individuals through the body of Christ, the Bride, then into all the world. Whether natural, supernatural, or personal gifting, all is stolen and lost by any person's untimely death.

All of us are created with a commitment to life. Harm is both instinctive and learned. As part of our "conscience," we have a line drawn in us that we know we should not cross. For instance, it is unnatural to cause human death, one's own or another's. When someone crosses this line and causes extreme harm or even death, it is as if something has fundamentally changed within them. Once done, it is easier to repeat. In a sense a person chooses to surrender himself to acts of murder, making it easier. Death and the power of harm, abuse, or bloodshed become part of us as we give ourselves over to them. Abuse of others becomes a little bit easier.

In Rwanda, the Hutu called the Tutsi snakes and cockroaches, and with this debased view of human nature it was not so difficult to kill them—"He is not a human being, he is a cockroach." Likewise, during earlier history, when the Tutsi were in power, one Tutsi chief talked about the Hutu being like pots—you can easily go and make other pots when some break. We find denial of human worth at the very heart of the genocide, denying both our own true humanity and that of others.

This chosen self-deceit must exist in us before we can harm another. One does not hesitate to stomp on a cockroach or a snake or a pot. We are describing here a process of dehumanization that ends in treating human beings like insects or discarded property. When such denial occurs at a national level it is profoundly dangerous, as we see from the history of Africa under the new Independence dictators of the 1960s (Meredith 2005).

Although human life has to be greatly devalued for genocide or any form of harm to occur, it is also further devalued by the act itself. If one person chooses to harm another, his own life is also devalued by the harm he does. By taking just one human life, all other human life, be it Hutu, Tutsi, or Twa, is devalued by the single act. A new threshold is reached where the individual is seen to be less than human. New "values" are written that then allow us to do more harm, injuring both God and others. Some say there is an intoxicating addictive pleasure to such behavior, and there must be for people to act in this way. But how much power does "evil" actually have?

Group Discussion Questions

1. What is your reaction to the undermining of traditional Rwandese values by the church and Colonialists?

2. How much is a human life worth?

3. Do you agree with the suggestion that God has a special love for children, the elderly, and the poor?

4. In what ways does modern society reflect these values?

5. In what ways can God's values be reflected in society today?

PART THREE

Africa, Genocide, and Evil

The issue of evil, or Evil if you want to personalize it, is a huge subject today. It is no longer confined to the pages of religious writings and theoretical journals. Many in modern society acknowledge the reality of evil in one sense or another. The daily news is continually reinforcing the awareness of its presence, while most of the time it is hidden in the fabric of society and people's actions.

In chapter 5, we introduced the concept of the serpent, a growing ideology of hate fed by a range of forces like jealousy, racism, and the need to provide for one's self and family. Such uncompromising racism was fed by education, the media, and, sadly, even religious leaders. This fed a pernicious evil that gripped people's lives and allowed them to do appalling things to others and themselves. The serpent lived.

In this book, we are going further than merely talking about evil. We are going to suggest that Evil is both personal and intentional. Our view, based on our experience of the damage in so many lives, is that evil is not merely random, but it has intelligence behind it and is strategically planned and intentionally malevolent. It is not just some value-neutral force that floats in the ether, but evil is a power to harm that somehow is able to assist and promote atrocious behavior through human beings as they choose to act.

But we are not suggesting that Evil goes unchecked. We are not suggesting it can do what it likes when it likes, snuffing out human life on a whim. Superficially, the genocide in Rwanda might give the impression this is possible, but what we are go-

ing to suggest is that Evil is subject to God in a number of ways, having expression only where human nature welcomes and promotes such evil.

In using Rwanda as a case study, we are intentionally seeking to be as explicit as we can about exposing this Evil and its intent. Without such a clear knowledge of any ground rules between God and the Enemy, it is difficult to understand what is going on in the world today. We are left feeling helpless and vulnerable, which is what many feel in Rwanda today. Instead, by studying such an extreme example of Evil at work, we will be able to extrapolate a range of simple and clear principles that are helpful to all of us in our own lives and societies and in our relationship with God. Also, these principles will help the Rwandese to know how such atrocities can be prevented.

CHAPTER 9

The Role of Evil

On January 26, 1999, PBS, a public TV channel in the U.S., broadcast a "frontline program," *The Rwanda Genocide: The Triumph of Evil.* Likewise Dallaire's book is entitled, *Shake Hands with the Devil.*[1] Both suggest a connection between human action and the presence of evil.

People freely speak of evil in genocide, even a personalized Evil and in practices like torture, carnage of a battlefield, child pornography/paedophilia, and abuse of the elderly, sick, and poor. What aspects of any genocide, the destruction of human life, are actually "evil"?

Human nature seems clearly capable of discerning evil, regardless of whether the person is Christian or not. People use the term *evil* freely to describe what is deeply unacceptable and offensive in human behavior. "He is evil." "What they did was evil." "Her behavior toward them was evil." But what people seem to also be saying in using this term is that somewhere in what they see or experience is an element that is more than merely human.[2]

The term *evil* is used to describe something that is out of character with normal human behavior. The suggestion is that some aspects of

---

1. Dallaire, *Shake Hands.*
2. But we would want to balance this emphasis with the plain fact that our brains' neurology is innately primed to not dislike people. D. Goleman, *Social Intelligence: The New Science of Human Relationship* (London: Hutchinson, 2006) 44, 54 ff.

human behavior are so appalling, as in the Rwandan genocide, they can only be described as super-human. In the term *evil* there is an implicit rejection that the actions are "just" human. Can human beings alone perpetrate such "evil"? Can it be merely human? As fellow human beings, we would like to reject such an idea.

By using the term *evil*, are we somehow suggesting that such atrocities must be more than merely the actions of human beings? The implication is that the people have somehow broken the constraints of humanity and have given themselves over to "evil," to its control and inspiration. To quote one of the killers from a BBC report, "It was as if we were taken over by Satan. When Satan is using you, you lose your mind. We were not ourselves. Beginning with me, I don't think I was normal."[3]

It is sometimes suggested that this is a temporary experience, with the person later confessing, "I didn't know what came over me." This claim has been the defense of many who have been accused. A typical example is a recorded conversation between a convicted genocidaire and Lesley Bilinda, speaking about her friend Anatolie: "Her death was unjust, senseless. She died for nothing. Even us, after we'd killed her and buried her, we were sad . . . we were all threatened . . . if you are from a mixed family what do you do in a time of war? You go with the stronger side, not the side that's being hunted."[4]

In this book, as in our ministries, we accept that evil power does exist, just as we accept that the much greater power of God also exists. There is plenty of evidence for both in the world around us, in Scripture, and in the lives of many we work with. However, we need to explore the question of how much power the Enemy really has. Is it as simple as saying that evil caused the genocide? How did such evil

---

3. <http://news.bbc.co.uk/1/hi/programmes/panorama/3562063.stm>.
4. L. Bilinda, *With What Remains: A Widow's Quest for Truth in Rwanda* (London: Hodder & Stoughton, 2006) 151.

come to be so powerful in the land of Rwanda? Does that evil "take you over"?

Evil in Society

We agree with Meeks that all people on earth share the experience of evil,[5] but in some regions it exhibits itself in worse ways than in others. Evil is particularly manifest in the shedding of human life. In Rwanda this racial hate was personified in a government-financed network, the *interahamwe*. In Kinyarwanda this word literally means "those who work together," a united force focused on one obsession, racial hate and murder of Tutsi and their sympathizers.

Between January 1993 and March 1994, the government imported more than 500,000 machetes, twice the number imported the previous year, one for every three adults. Stockpiles of arms, grenades, machetes, and axes were stored in *communes* all over the country. Also, extensive lists were drawn up of all those who should be slaughtered. Each *interahamwe commune* was made up of around forty men, and the UN was told by a defector, Jean-Pierre Twatsinze, that these militia had been trained to kill up to one thousand Tutsi and their sympathizers in twenty minutes (Meredith 2005.503).

What we see is a cynical national government policy of systematic extermination of Rwandan citizens. The Rwandan government's genocidal policy was also supported by countries like France (Meredith 2005.519). President Mitterrand was a friend of Habyarimana, then president of Rwanda. The French even supplied the Falcon jet and three French crew members who were shot down, so igniting the genocide.

But aside from the Kayibanda/Habyarimana regime, the French were not the only guilty party. For instance, the Belgian ambassador reported a build up of a government sponsored militia in the spring of 1992, and a CIA analysis in January 1994 predicted the failure of

---

5. W. A. Meeks, *The Origins of Christian Morality: The First Two Centuries* (New Haven: Yale University Press, 1993) 129.

the Arusha Accord, which would then open the way to mass slaughter of at least half a million targeted people (Meredith 2005.503). It did just that, even taking precedent over fear of God. A person about to be murdered in the genocide asked the *interahamwe*, "Would you please give me time for prayer?" Their killers responded that they had killed God first.

For a human being to kill another, especially in such a callous way, something must first die in the killer. Imagine if your wife is a Tutsi and in order to prove you are a loyal militant you must either kill her or open the door for others to kill her. You have no choice or you and your children will be killed. The seeds of the action may well have been sown over many years through the dark ideology of racism and hate. But when you kill, when you destroy human life, that death impacts you, too.[6]

So any theology of genocide must also ask what role the evil might play in this process and how it might promote such human slaughter. People instinctively turn to evil as a reason for explaining how such terrible things happen. Some even seek to blame an evil power that "caused" the devastation. In the case of the Rwandan genocide, one sees numerous references to general evil and also to the Enemy. An example is Major General Dallaire,[7] who, when confronted with unmitigated evil, refused to ignore it:[8] "I had to negotiate with the devil. I talked to him, laughed, and maneuvered with him . . . I know there's a God because I negotiated with his enemy."[9]

---

6. Some have found that this experience of being tainted by death is something that they feel if they have had an abortion. Part of my (Peter's) work is to help men and women find healing from such encounters with death.

7. Dallaire, *Shake Hands*.

8. M. Joseph, *Seeking the Sacred: Leading a Spiritual Life in a Secular World* (Ontario: ECW Press, 2006) 9.

9. R. Dallaire, "Trial, the Struggle," in *Seeking the Sacred: Leading a Spiritual Life in a Secular World*, ed. M. Joseph (Ontario: ECW Press, 2006) 43–62.

Genocide is spiritual as well as physical fratricide, the killing of one's brothers and sisters. When speaking of such slaughter, people spontaneously associate such acts with a driven demonic evil.[10] When human life is taken, it can release a wave of evil and a sense of darkness that leaves one with the impression that evil power is total, that darkness prevails over life, and that Satan and his hoards have unchecked power over anyone or anything they wish to destroy.

We have both witnessed circumstances where people have been overwhelmed by evil hate, the consequences of lust for human blood that the Enemy can unleash when human life is unrighteously taken. We both understand how people can get so caught up as victims in such human carnage that they then can no longer find God, especially a God of love. Coming out of such an experience one is left asking a tirade of questions: Where was God? Why did He not stop it? How could He have allowed such a thing? One feels God is impotent when the Enemy decides to randomly take human life. Satan feels more powerful, while God is merely a spectator to such things.[11] Finding God subsequently—His solace, love, and peace—is a beautiful journey of release and recovery.

The Destruction of Human Life as Revenge to God

On the assumption that such an evil exists, we must ask ourselves how much power evil really has. But before doing so, let us look first at the intent of evil. In some ways the intention is obvious, but looking at the obvious is often a very helpful step in building our understanding of events and situations.

---

10. One of the most shocking aspects for the authors is that some even today advocate and celebrate genocide and the associated worship of Satan. See www.evilmusic. com and bands like Black Metal, Oi!, RAC, Death Metal, and <www.paganfront. com>.
11. For one remarkable and beautiful account of a woman's journey with God through the genocide, see I. Llibagiza, *Left to Tell: One Woman's Story of Surviving the Rwandan Holocaust* (London: Hay House, 2006).

Satan, the Enemy, hates God, so the Enemy lusts to destroy what God has created and finds good (Genesis 1:31). Also, because men and women are made in God's image, were he able to, the Enemy would want to destroy human life, wherever it exists on earth. Although, it seems unlikely that Satan's purposes are always ultimately fulfilled in merely promoting massive destruction of human life.

One aspect of the Enemy's pleasure seems to be in human suffering, alongside death, murder, self-destruction, and all its related abuse of human beings by themselves and by others. Every opportunity to abuse what God created is an opportunity to take revenge on God. The destruction of human life, causing the pain of grief to God,[12] seems to give the Enemy pleasure.

When darkness or evil wants to take revenge on God, how can it be done? Explains Genesis 6:6: "The Lord was grieved that he had made man on earth. And his heart was filled with pain." God felt pain because of the exercise and exploitation of human sin. His love for His creation, how good things were intended to be, makes God especially vulnerable to His human creation. As it is for human beings, so it is for God. Things that we love most can be the things that can most hurt us. On this basis, if the enemy is able to promote evil behavior through people as they embrace that evil and its subsequent harm of human life, then the Enemy will be able to pain God. Loss of all kinds is painful to both human beings and to God.[13]

The idea that human beings can do serious harm to themselves and others is clearly noted in Scripture. Two key texts that support this idea are Genesis 6:5 and 11–12: "The Lord saw how great man's wickedness on the earth had become, and that every inclination of the thoughts of his heart was only evil all the time . . . The earth was corrupt in God's

---

12. For a range of classic quotes on the suffering of God, see R. A. Kauffman, "Suffering God," *Christianity Today* (2007) 71.

13. We are both exploring the idea of writing a book around the theme of a biblical theology of loss in a Rwandan setting.

sight and was full of violence . . . for all the people on earth had corrupted their ways." And Genesis 8:21: "The LORD smelled the pleasing aroma and said in his heart: 'Never again will I curse the ground because of man, even though every inclination of his heart is evil from childhood.'"

Damaged human nature clearly has the capacity to work with the Enemy against God. This disturbingly negative view of human nature is not just confined to the Old Testament, but it is also a view endorsed by Christ (Matthew 15:16–20; 16:4). So, the Enemy has a big advantage in the sense that, from God's perspective, human nature has a natural propensity to harm. People find it easier to do wrong than right, or harder to do good than to plan evil. This is self-evident in that from childhood we must all *learn* to do what is right and true. We seem to naturally do wrong.

But the ultimate hurt against God perpetrated by human beings is something far worse than bad behavior. We have already noted that murder arrived on the scene in the earliest chapters of Genesis, the shedding of the blood of Abel by Cain. The death of Abel and the cry of his shed blood are heard by the Lord. "Where is your brother Abel?" "Am I my brother's keeper?" "Your brother's blood cries out to me from the ground. Now you are under a curse and driven from the ground" (Genesis 4:9–11).

From the earliest pages of Scripture, we see that God notices the unjust shedding of blood, and we see His role in avenging such acts. What we read here is that the blood of murdered people, and their shattered lives, cries out to the throne room of heaven. This increases God's pain. This open honesty in God tells us that to pain God you have to act like Cain in either sinning, or more extremely in taking human life in an unjust and untimely way. The Giver of life witnesses the destruction of life. Those He has given life, those made in His image, have participated in destroying what He has created.

Two fronts are being opened here. The Enemy has his own hidden agenda of sacrificing human life where and when he can, aided by human sin. But we are also looking at fallen human nature and the tragic breakdown of people's values where people harm one another, even by torture and murder.

The Enemy's Power in Scripture

Some may speak of an "uncontrollable evil" or the "indescribable carnage of human life." These phrases, combined with the horror and fear of experiencing such trauma, attribute significant power to the Enemy. It is important to put all this in the context of Scripture.

The Bible tells us that it is God we need to fear. He is the one with whom all authority rests. We do not see an all-powerful Enemy, wreaking havoc wherever he chooses. The Enemy's power seems limited by God. Otherwise grace would not prevail. So how do we reconcile the evil we see in the world around us with the truth that is in Scripture? Several principles are helpful in contextualizing our understanding of what can happen in the spiritual landscape, both from God's and the Enemy's perspective.

First, Satan answers directly to Christ (Colossians 2:10). We need to remember this. When we are faced with tragic devastation, it is all too easy to forget that Satan is merely an angel, not an equal with Christ. The false suggestion of book titles like *Between Christ and Satan*, suggesting an equality of two spiritual powers, can deceive us. Biblically, this is not the case with Christ and Satan. Christ as God is far superior to any of his created angels.[14] In answering to Christ, the Enemy is subject to Him.

Second, and following this first principle, it seems from Scripture that the Enemy's powers are limited by two constraints. One is what Christ permits, and the other is what human beings choose to do.

---

14. For a helpful modern view of this, see N. G. Wright, *A Theology of the Dark Side: Putting the Power of Evil in Its Place* (Carlisle: Paternoster Press, 2003).

Comments Paul Wood, "The riot in Ephesus illustrates this point in Scripture (Acts 19). The crowds are drawn out in support of their fertility goddess, Artemis, who was no doubt feeling threatened by the repentance from occult practices. Most people would not have known why they were there, but would have been 'stirred up' by the moment. But human nature does not have to respond in this compelling way."

Along similar lines, the temptations of Christ (Matthew 4) illustrate that the Enemy clearly has the power to tempt people (1 Corinthians 7:5), but as Christ demonstrated, human nature can resist if it so chooses. This suggests that the Enemy is unable to do anything that would be classified as being forced on humankind. For the Enemy to have his way, a person must first cooperate (see Judas in John 13:27). People can and do resist the temptation of harming themselves or others.

As an example a person being tempted and resisting, Satan clearly sought to mislead Peter (Mark 8:33; Luke 22:31), but his attempts failed. He seems unable to force his demonic wishes on human beings when they choose to refuse. He is sly, seeking to outwit us (2 Corinthians 2:11), and he even masquerades as righteousness (2 Corinthians 11:4). Following Satan always remains a free choice for human beings (Acts 26:16; 1 Timothy 5:15). People do not have to learn his so-called "deep secrets" if they do not want to (1 John 5:19; Revelation 2:24). Nonetheless, like Cain, human beings can choose to surrender to this evil and act accordingly (1 John 3:12–13). Some would describe this process as "turning that part of me [that can feel pity or guilt] off."[15]

The Enemy's powers are therefore limited by both Christ (Zechariah 3; Revelation 20:2) and by human free will. Restraining grace from God seems to prevail, since human life today continues to prevail on the earth. But when human life is taken, it does unleash a

15. Goleman, *Social Intelligence*, 117.

sense of the power of evil, so all people have a tendency to attribute the evil to Satan rather than to human action. It seems to be in human nature always to seek to pass the blame—it is never our fault! The Enemy becomes a convenient person to blame.

Third, it is not only Scripture that suggests Satan is not all-powerful. The evidence from human history seems to suggest that although the harming of human beings is a delight to the Enemy, his powers to do so are somewhat limited. Pleasure in the power to destroy human life is certainly demonically supported, but the simple evidence that the majority of us go unscathed during our full cycle of life suggests that the Enemy does not have uncontrolled power to hurt and destroy all human life. One needs to find a balance, both theologically and personally, between the Enemy's lust to destroy and God's restraining grace.

The fourth and perhaps most disturbing principle is that although Satan's power is limited, the evidence of human experience seems to suggest that Satan and his hordes can support, exploit, and facilitate human misbehavior. Satan cannot impose an action on human beings where they do not wish to surrender to it, but he will lend strength to human will when it is turned against the purposes of God. The tone of Scripture, and the nature of the Enemy's relationship with Christ and human beings, suggests that Satan and his demonic hosts seem dependent, to some degree, on human cooperation, as was the case for Judas, the Sanhedrin (John 18:14), and Pilate (John 18:28) in the case of crucifying Christ. The Enemy needs human cooperation in order to "enjoy" the pleasure of hurting a human life.

Although the Enemy seems to have the power of (premature) death (Hebrews 2:14), the existence of so many people on the earth today illustrates that it is clearly limited in some ways that are not yet fully understood by us. The line blurs between human action and demonic action. They are both clearly complicit. This is what we will explore more fully in our next chapter.

We suggest therefore that a flaw of both western Christianity and people generally is to attribute more power to Satan than he is truly able to achieve without human assistance. The proliferation and persistent well being of human life on earth prove this point. If human beings did not cooperate with Satan's plans, he would have even less power in material reality. Therefore, in any social theology of genocide, we must acknowledge the satanic in the background or spiritual landscape of any human carnage. But we should be careful to avoid the suggestion that genocide is demonically initiated or forced on human beings by the Enemy. Human will and action seems to be able to prevail, even while recognizing that the human heart, from the beginning of Scripture, is desperately wicked (see Genesis 6:5, 11; 8:21).

People must have the freedom of choice to act on their will to be accountable to the law, to society, and to God. If they deny they have a will, they are less than human. Therefore, the human will is important, for it gives people the power to do good or the power to do evil. To say we are not responsible for what we do, as some people try to do, is to deny our humanity, to deny our free will to choose. People may regret what they have done, but they cannot deny that they had a choice, the will to participate in the act. Free will is a gift from God for all of us. But how we use it is our choice.

Group Discussion Questions

1. How do you feel about the idea that the Enemy takes revenge on God by harming human beings?

2. Do you believe in personal Evil, a Satan?

3. To what extent, and how, can people resist evil?

4. Do you agree with Paul Wood that "human nature does not have to respond in this compelling way" to commit evil?

5. Do you see from Scripture any support for the claim that "the Enemy made me do it"?

6. What is your reaction to the idea that the Enemy demands the shedding of human blood? How should we respond?

CHAPTER 10

Human Personal Evil and the Demonic

We are noting that individuals have free choice, either to cooperate with the intention of the Enemy or to resist him. But we have also seen that the Enemy will seek, shrewdly and subtly, to take revenge on God and destroy everything good, precipitating maximum hate, pain, and death. So how is it that human beings, created by God and in relationship with Him, can turn away and cooperate with the Enemy's intent to destroy all that is human and beautiful?

In many of the most traumatic situations of the twentieth century, we saw a minority of people collaborating with a small leadership to bring about mass murder. In the Holocaust for example, the death camps were kept secret. The majority of Germans, though perhaps guilty of ignoring the blatant racism, were not aware of the extent of the "ethnic cleansing" in their midst. But this was not the case in Rwanda.

"Ordinary," peace-loving people became murderers overnight, inadvertently aided and abetted by an international community that watched as tens of thousands were slaughtered every day. How can such a thing really happen? We are going to look at three areas: what happens when the Enemy takes advantage of our choices, what happens in the special case of violent or premature human death, and more unusually, what happens when children are killed.

Addiction to Power and to Blood

The *Gacaca* court is part of a system of community justice inspired by tradition and established in 2001 in Rwanda. The court determined that there were three levels of personal involvement in the 1994 genocide: those who planned and led the genocide, those who saw the potential for economic gain and took advantage of it, and those who were carried along by the slaughter. The first two types clearly involve intent, a calculated choice repeated over time. But the third type involved a more spontaneous act, albeit one that lasted for a month or longer. Some weeks before, and perhaps after the event, a person in this category had no wish to be involved in such massacre again. But in the heat of the moment, he too took up weapons, killing and maiming.

From the accounts of those who were caught up in the murders, it is clear that some became addicted by the power to harm and to the hate and the shedding of human blood. We are not referring here to those who planned the genocide. Their intent was far more deliberate, calculated, purposeful. But for some of the men and women who suddenly found themselves with blood on their hands and weapons at their side, there was a surprising addiction to do more. When they felt the power, the release of the hate, they were more easily able to do it again. Others went into deep and profound shock, and for years afterward they loathed the time they committed such atrocities.

But it is in this addictive state that people say, "I don't know what came over me." They became capable of acts that normally would have repulsed them. One of the shocking things about the 1994 genocide in Rwanda is the extreme level of torture and deliberately inflicted pain, even on those about to be murdered. Instead of a simple mass slaughter, men, women, and children were forced to endure horrific suffering before being left to die or, perhaps more mercifully, being killed.

We are suggesting that human nature enjoys sin. This is shockingly illustrated in the many reports of assassins killing their fellow human beings with machetes, knives, and spears while laughing hysterically. They enjoyed seeing people suffer and the power they had to hurt them. They enjoyed the fear their power provoked. They laughed at the trauma they inflicted. They became addicted to the power of shedding human blood. The power, the blood, and the pain became intoxicating.

One must also concede that a depraved imagination is behind such pernicious destructive evil. Would human nature alone normally be able to concoct such evil? If not, human beings have an ally, and the evidence speaks eloquently of the ultimate nature and goal of this dark angel and his followers. His evil lust to destroy human life has no bounds except God Himself (Matthew 24:21).

Demonically Driven Human Choices

What many people believe is that the practice of such "evil" acts requires that one be "possessed" by something more powerful than one's self. Human action becomes dictated by or driven by something supranormal. This seems to be the experience of some people in the gospels (Mark 9:14; Luke 4:31), though not to the extent of committing genocide.

The evidence of Christ is that the demonic is predatory (Luke 22:31–32), seeking to exploit either the sin (Matthew 9:1–8) or disorder in people's lives (Mark 9:41; Luke 11:24–26) and on occasions physically trying to hurt them (Mark 9:20; Luke 4:35). Sometimes this "possession" seems to be long-term (Matthew 17:14; Mark 5:1–5), while it can also be an occasional event (Luke 9:37–40). This is why many Christians today would make a distinction between oppression by the Enemy (the occasional) and possession (long-term). In its extreme form, a chosen surrender to the Enemy can be worship of the Enemy (Revelation 9:20–21).

How does this oppression or possession occur in otherwise well-intentioned individuals? It seems to be by their own personal choice, building over a period of time. It is each person's choice to take the opportunity, to take advantage of the power given, each one's choice to hate or to harm. These gradual steps toward greater harm to others gives more strength and opportunity to the Enemy. This was how Satan entered Judas (John 13:27) and tried to enter Peter (Mark 8:33)—promising the power to harm.

One talks about being "possessed" by the Enemy or his hoards. Consequently, the acts themselves, with all their "evil" obsessions, are driven by the demonic, but they are done through human behavior—both in deliberation and consequences. What becomes clear, even in a brief overview of the subject of the demonic, is that Satan himself seeks to exploit human sin and misbehavior, and where he can he will support and promote any and all forms of human misbehavior. Oppression and possession do not seem to imply a person being taken over and, in a robotic way, being used to kill and harm. People can, if they wish, resist this predatory exploitation (Mark 16:15; James 4:7), or they can choose to give themselves over to its power (Matthew 9:28; 11:24; Luke 4:33).[1]

Christ taught that only He is permitted to possess human beings. We should not only be clothed in Christ but also have Him live in us (John 14:23; 17:26). But in a similar way, human beings appear to have the power to surrender themselves to spirits other than the Holy Spirit and become possessed by them. The person, once possessed by such evil spirits, can act in ways that are supernormal (Mark 5:4). The slaughter of human life, done by human beings, is therefore ultimately attributed to Satan (Revelation 11:7–10; 12:9). In this possessed state, human beings are able to perform evil acts both against themselves and others (Genesis 4:6–7; Revelation 9:18).

---

1. But we would also want to clarify the erosion of free will by habitual sin, addiction, and an unwillingness to own our baggage.

Scripture does not seem to show evidence of a direct connection between the role of evil actually imposing human suffering and the specific carnage that is part of our human history in this world. Even though the Enemy may wish to claim such powers over people, Scripture is silent on this direct connection. Instead, Scripture merely recognizes the place of human evil and its power to take life (see, for instance, Genesis 6:5, 11; 8:21). Scripture does not seek to explain how this works.

But in making human beings responsible for acts of evil, a caution is needed. Christ acknowledges the Enemy's power to steal fruit (Matthew 13:19). Christ also calls Satan a murderer from the beginning, suggesting *he* was behind the murder of Abel by Cain. Christ states: "You belong to your father, the devil, and you want to carry out your father's desire. He was a murderer from the beginning" (John 8:44). Christ attributes this death and its power to Satan, even though one sees no direct biblical evidence that Satan has directly murdered anyone. Instead, we need to admit that the Enemy's instrument always seems to be people.

Christ's statement is important to all of us, because it notes the dualism of what one person did to another while acknowledging that in the spiritual landscape of the events there was a participatory responsibility of the Enemy's purposes as well. What Christ seems to be suggesting is that none of us are robots, neither are we merely clay molded by the Enemy, who can make us do whatever he wants. If this were true, there would be no such thing as the gift of free human will, a gift from God for all of us that is integral to our humanness.

Instead, our own actions and choices can be supplemented by the power of the Enemy. We, perhaps unwittingly, become part of the means by which he achieves his purposes. This leads us to the conclusion that while the genocide was no doubt demonically empowered, the initial planning and the individual choices were all human.

Human Death

The issue of death itself in Scripture is also an interesting one. The Enemy has the power of death (Hebrews 2:14). This would suggest the power in certain situations to kill prematurely, though Scripture does not seem to expand on how this power was given and how it is practiced. Scripture also teaches that the timely death of followers of Christ, at a time chosen by God, is sweet to God: "Precious in the sight of the Lord is the death of his saints" (Psalm 116:15). On this basis God must feel grief when a life is taken prematurely, as with murder, suicide, genocide, or even "accidents." Untimely death is where God's promise of a long life is not fulfilled (Ecclesiastes 8:15; John 5:21), where life is stolen.

Although evil often seems to be behind human misbehavior, it does not seem to be able to force or induce such human harm without human surrender. Human evil alone seems to be enough to perform murder, without the direct addition of the demonic (Genesis 18:20–21; 19:4). Jesus even suggests that others will murder Christians in the name of God during the last days (John 16:1–4). So although it seems a human instinct to attribute "evil" to unacceptable human acts, it is not accurate to give Satan and his hoards full credit for extreme harmful behavior by human beings. People may call it evil, but it could just be human evil behavior. On the other hand, the Enemy could be behind it. We cannot tell. It may be that only the gift of discernment will help us to know the difference (Hebrews 5:11–14).

We believe a note a caution is needed. Although people recognize a direct connection between human atrocities and their demonic inspiration or support, it will not be until the return of Christ that such matters are finally settled (see Matthew 13: 49–50; 16:27; 24:3; 25:14–4). Then we will see more clearly what is human and what is demonic in the fabric of human history. Likewise, at present we are unable to understand clearly how such demonically inspired evil actually takes place and what the mechanics of this process actually are. It is not possible at this time to say how this actually happens.

But what is clear is that, both from Scripture and people's experience, one can see a direct connection between the destruction of human life, including children, and the inspiration of the Enemy in exploiting and promoting such human behavior. But one must be careful not to attribute to Satan what one human being does to another. In the case of the Rwandan genocide, many people were killed by fellow citizens, friends, family, and neighbors. How can a man kill his wife and children as an act of racism? To what extent can we blame the person, and at what point do we blame the Enemy? At this time we seem unable to conclusively answer where the line can be drawn.

Human Child Sacrifice

Although not a central focus of Scripture, the references to child sacrifice have a telling message for us today. God forbids such sacrifice: "Do not give any of your children to be sacrificed to Molech" (Leviticus 18:21). The death penalty was imposed on any Israelite who did (Leviticus 20).[2] But as Solomon grew old, his foreign wives turned his heart to worship Molech, causing his descendents to lose the kingdom (1 Kings 11:4). Yahweh describes Molech as "that detestable god" (1 Kings 11:5). Josiah desecrated some of the high places used for child sacrifice (2 Kings 23:10), while Jeremiah condemned such sacrifices (Jeremiah 32:35) and later sent Molech into exile (Jeremiah 49:3).[3]

Evil power is attached to the idea of child sacrifice. Something demonic is released when a child is killed in this ritualistic way. Let us illustrate. When the king of Edom was losing his battle against Israel,

---

2. While asserting strongly God's hatred of child sacrifice, we would also want to distinguish this from the sacrifice of Christ, which was clearly undertaken with the Father's approval. (Thank you to Canon Michael Green for this point.)
3. For a full discussion of the subject of Molech, see G. C. Heider, "Molech," in *The Dictionary of Deities and Demons in the Bible*, ed. K. V. D. Toorn, et al. (Leiden: Brill, 1995) 1090.

he took his eldest son, who was to inherit his throne, and killed him on the city wall. "The fury against Israel was great; they withdrew and returned to their own land" (2 Kings 3:26). Israel was defeated by the shedding of the child's blood and the evil it subsequently released against them.

Something horrific is discharged by the ritual shedding of innocent blood, especially that of children. Scripture is silent on how this works, but it seems to be the case. A demonic authority is somehow unleashed when blood is shed in this way. In studying some of the ways children were killed in Rwanda, a ritual symbolism is mirrored in some of these killings. The impact on the surviving abused mother alone would be devastating.

One should be careful not to overlook the close parallels between what the Enemy demanded of pagan kings fighting Israel, and some of the consequences that may have been felt or released by the crazed evil done against the children in Rwanda.[4] The evidence is that such slaughter released more evil, which in turn led to much more slaughter. Only the intervention of the police and a damping down of this excessive evil brought it to an end.

When looking at Scripture on child sacrifice, one must put this pagan evil practice into perspective. What Scripture also speaks of is a greater sacrifice. In fact, the greatest sacrifice. This is the giving of Christ, the Son, by the Father (Hebrews 7:27). This greater sacrifice is the foundation of our own salvation and holiness. Shedding of human blood is no longer needed, especially the sacrifice of children. Instead we should affirm the death, resurrection, and atoning of Christ. The shedding of His blood brings an end to the shedding of blood. Comments Paul Wood, "To deal with and redeem the blood-soaked

---

4. It still continues. See *The New Times,* KIGALI, September 21, 2006, page 5, "Woman arrested for cannibalism," where a twenty-three-year-old killed a five-year-old girl, a neighbor, cut off her legs, and with a friend cooked and ate them, throwing the rest of the body away. They were told by an old woman to do this if they wanted to end their personal troubles.

land would seem to be critical to giving the people of Rwanda a safe place to find their healing."

Group Discussion Questions

1. What are your views on possession by the Enemy?

2. How would you distinguish between possession by the Enemy and Christ in us?

3. Why do we need the gift of discernment to see evil?

4. What does Scripture teach about the role of evil in the world and how can we resist it?

5. Outline some ways that we see evil in the world today.

CHAPTER 11

The East African
Great Lakes Region

Introducing Africa

Africa has the dubious distinctions of having some of the harshest climates, largest populations, and poorest societies on earth. Africa has a rapidly growing population of more than five hundred million and the highest birth-rate of any continent. It has over one thousand language groups and many more dialects and cultural-regional distinctions. Some of the largest deserts and the richest farmland are in Africa. It has some of the greatest lakes and some of the most polluted rivers. Africa is a remarkable continent for many reasons.

Nestled in the highlands of Central East Africa is a small country barely the size of Maryland (U.S.) or Belgium. It is rich in vegetation and has consistent seasonal rainfall that makes it one of the most productive farmland regions in Africa.

This beautiful, lush green landscape has been the backdrop for the worst genocide, the worst single outbreak of mass destruction in Africa. It is as if alongside this majestic landscape has been placed a spiritual scenery in which the serpent we described earlier has been exerting its influence—sometimes seen, sometimes hidden.

We have already noted that the racist hate in the region was fed by the colonial settlers. So what of the spiritual scenery prior to that time? Is there a bigger picture here than any of us have been aware of? In this chapter we want to suggest some ideas that might contribute to an understanding of the prevalence of genocide in all the East African nations. They are speculations that might be helpful in gaining a deeper understanding of the spiritual landscape of the genocide.

Pre-Christian Religion of the Region

Here are the questions many people ask: "Isn't the Great Lakes area a Christian region?[1] So why are all these atrocities happening there?" It is true that the Great Lakes Region of Rwanda, Burundi, Tanzania, Congo, and Uganda is 90 percent Christian. They are Christian countries, so what has happened?

In Africa the spiritual landscape is all about ancient and often forgotten covenants. Ancestors made commitments to a variety of gods, commitments that are now forgotten or ignored. But if we accept that such spiritual powers do exist, if we treat these gods as part of the spiritual landscape, then we must ask what the consequences are of these covenants that were made. Are they really forgotten, along with the people who made them? Or do they still exist and carry authority in the spiritual landscape until they are renounced?

---

1. The official figure is that Muslims represent only a very small minority of the population, and the majority played no active part in the genocide. Peter and Kibalama (eds.), *Civil Society*, 43.

Let us look at an example. It is known that in these regions worship of river, lake, and forest gods used to be common practice.[2] This worship involved appeasing the gods, sometimes involving the shedding of blood, animal or human. Worshipers would make covenants, promises that they would fulfill, so that the gods in return would look favorably on the people who depended, for example, on the fish of the lake for their livelihood. Before the coming of the missionaries the shedding of blood in sacrifice was common in the region.

In Rwandan society there was no direct worship of the rivers or lakes apart from its connection with the ancestors. And there was no human sacrifice. But if the native peoples of the region had made covenants with the gods, what would happen to those covenants once the ancestral gods were no longer being worshiped? From the time Christianity reached the Great Lakes Region, the practice of human or blood sacrifice was outlawed. Such covenants have stood for centuries. So are we to assume that simply by the coming of the missionaries and the building of churches they are annulled?

It is possible to imagine that in the Great Lakes Region the ancient river gods are still demanding shed blood in fulfilment of these covenants. Is it their right? The arrival of Christianity, far from annulling the covenants, would starve them of fulfillment. Thereafter the "account" was not being balanced. The claim of these gods, particularly of the lakes, rivers, and forests, were therefore not being met. But the ancient covenants still stood. Perhaps in the genocide we see the claims of these covenants being redressed, with blood being shed.

---

2. For background to the water god culture of North East Africa, see T. Allen, "Understanding Alice: Uganda's Holy Spirit Movement in Context," *Africa* 61 (1991) 3; E. Ludwig, *The Nile: The Life Story of a River*, George Allen and Unwin Ltd, 1940), D. Ogungbile, "Water Symbolism in African Culture and Afro Christian Churches," *Journal of Religious Thought* 53/54 (1997) 21; F. E. Prins, "Praise to the Bushmen Ancestors of the Water," in *Miscast: Negotiating the Presence of the Bushmen*, ed. P. Skotnes (Cape Town University Press, 1996); B. Shadle, "Patronage, Millenialism and the Serpent God Mumbo in South-West Kenya," *Africa* 72 (2002) 29. (Thanks to Paul Wood.)

Comments Paul Wood, "I would suggest, intuitively, that there were (and still are) ancient issues of the land and the water, covenants made with human blood, that the revival was intended to penetrate and exorcise. But for whatever reason it was stopped short of that. [The country of] Wales shows us that if revival stops short the condition afterward can be worse than before. The stopping short has much to do with human and institutional control, so the church is the key player."

For much of the last century these blood covenants were not being met. In 1994, the river Kagera, the "river of blood," was blocked with the dead bodies of the people slaughtered. The rivers ran red and took many thousands of the dead bodies down into Lake Victoria. One way of looking at this is that in the spiritual landscape, the neglect of human sacrifice was being redressed.

During the genocide some people were given the job of killing babies. It is blasphemy against the Christian God to kill a baby, to destroy purity and innocence. Likewise, women were dehumanized, paraded publicly, and raped. Pregnant women were opened up to see if the baby was a boy, so it could be killed. Every male (Tutsi and moderate Hutu) that could be found was killed. Was this also echoing the traditional demands of the gods, the spirits of the jungle and the hills, and the water gods of the Nilotic and Lakes Region? Such practices take us back to the times of Moses, Egypt, and the Pharaoh's (Exodus 11), or even to the time of Christ's birth, where all male babies were ordered to be killed (Matthew 2:16).

Blood Covenants

Connected to this is the practice of eating human flesh and drinking the blood. It is traditionally believed in African society that when one has the opportunity to do this then the person's spirit will not come after you. This is especially true if you are able to eat the heart. These practices were supposed to be a guaranteed way to stop people from coming back from the spirit world and avenging you. It is said that Idi

Amin, who committed appalling atrocities in Uganda, would wipe his mouth with the bloodied sword with which he had killed people.

We are noting a belief in the power of the sharing of shed blood. Pacts between individuals who wanted to strengthen their relationship involved blood covenants, often including a ritual and witnesses. This was part of African culture. Such traditions were widely accepted, giving rights to family member. A simple illustration of this is two people using a razor and cutting their abdomens, then each putting the other's blood in his own mouth. As this is done, someone else pronounces words over both, stating that if they betray the covenant grave misfortune will fall on both them and their families.

It is interesting to go deeper, by noting the similarity between some practices in traditional African religion and those of the Old Testament. Blood symbolized life, the life in the body. In the Old Testament, it was the practice to lay the sins of the people on the goat. The goat's life became the vehicle of shame for removing sin from among the people (Leviticus 16:5). In Africa, in a similar way, they lay the curses on the goats or other animals. Or they capture the spirits of the deceased person in a pot and put it somewhere in the forest. You are warned not to touch or go near the pot, or the spirit will come after you. Likewise, when you see a wandering goat you will always avoid it.

A Christian Response

To the ears of those in the West, a spirituality that believes in river gods, covenants of worship, and the power of shed blood is so far removed from daily life that it may almost sound ridiculous. If we are to support Rwanda as it recovers from this genocide, if we are to help the people recover the best of their values and traditions, it is important that we understand the world they are familiar with. It is not for us to decide that the way they see material and spiritual realities is folly. Perhaps they understand more than we do what the connections really are. The deepest deceptive power of the Enemy is in his ability to stop us owning truth about ourselves and the world we all live in. What we deny becomes his hidden power.

Christianity traditionally, somewhat arrogantly, has a tendency to ignore the blood covenants of ancient peoples and presumes that the blood of Christ automatically clears it all away when it moves into an area and plants churches. The evidence may be that these ancient rituals and their covenants still stand and continue to have some authority. This would go some way to explain the pogrom of bloodshed in this region. We have already noted the connection between evil and human cooperation. It may be that unless these covenants are now specifically undone and renounced, they will quietly remain in place, demanding more bloodshed.

Such hidden covenants are a deep challenge to the church. For instance, in Uganda even today some people go down to the lakes to connect with spirits there. This happens at all the lakes. The spirits are believed to be in the lakes, and it is said they are very stubborn and demanding.

It is also interesting to note that one of the things Yahweh did at the time of the Exodus was to drown the Egyptian army in the river, thereby proving He was stronger than the Egyptian Nilotic river gods. Yahweh has more authority. If the church ignores these ancestral claims, does that weaken the authority of Christ in the same way that Israel was weakened when it did not deal with other gods in the way Yahweh required?

In traditional African society when men went to war, it is said the mother held her right breast, thereby sending the men away with a blessing so they return conquerors, having shed the blood of the enemy. One of the problems may be that Christianity has largely ignored many of these rituals and practices of the indigenous local people of the region. This could mean that Christianity is no more than a cultural veneer, with much of this ancient covenant history remaining untouched and unchallenged.

Group Discussion Questions

1. Where in Scripture do we see the importance of blood covenants?

2. Can women be blamed for remaining silent when their men were genocidaires?

3. Did the church do wrong in ignoring these ancient beliefs of the people of the Great Lakes Region?

4. What is your reaction to the idea that some of these ancient covenants might still have power today? What do you think the church should do about this?

CHAPTER 12

Violence Against Women and Children

Traditional Rwandan society would not allow women, children, or the elderly to be harmed, even in times of war, for "their blood is dangerous." Children were innocent, women the source of life, and the elderly the source of wisdom. Society cannot be sustained without their wisdom. These values were all part of traditional African society, except in the 1994 genocide. This brings us into the greatest depths of evil, an evil lusting for the destruction of the lives of those least able to defend themselves. The slaughter of women and children reflects how deep the depravity of human nature can actually fall. There seems no historic parallel to the extent of the Rwandan genocide targeting, abusing, and slaying women and children. Even in the Nazi Holocaust one saw the murder of children, but not on this scale.

The evidence also says something about the ultimate focus of both the demonic and the leaders of the genocide, its lust to destroy the two most significant givers of life for men: his women and children. Taking these away from him breaks the man in the same way that it has broken the nation.

Theologically, the mounting evidence regarding the torture, amputations, maiming, and abuse of women and children also speaks of the "total depravity" not only of human nature but also of the profligate evil of the mind of the Enemy. Humans have to imagine a thing before they can actually do it.[1] They rehearse it. It is therefore profoundly disturbing to concede that human nature would have rehearsed such sick and depraved behavior before it actually did the deeds.

What we have suggested is that the Enemy can do something even worse than merely taking people's lives. Instead, it is the ultimate capacity of the Enemy to offend God in the death of whole groups of people.[2] Society now describes this process as genocide. But we are also noting that because children, the elderly, and the poor have a special place in the heart of God (see Deuteronomy 15:11; Luke 14:13; James 2:5), they are inevitably a specific target of the Enemy. Genocide against children has got to be the very worst affront to God.

I (Emmanuel) have two particularly difficult problems with the 1994 genocide. One is killing so many children, and the other is raping and abusing women. Let us address these issues specifically.

The Murder of Women

Why were so many women and children killed and women targeted for rape and sexual abuse? It seems to have been the direct policy of the militias, or *interahamwe,* either to kill or to infect women with HIV and to focus physical and sexual abuse on women's breasts and genitalia. In noting such a strategy, one needs to ask what the spiritual landscape might be of such appalling behavior? One suggestion we are in some sympathy with is the idea that the Enemy carries a singular hateful jealousy of women, because unlike the Enemy himself or his demonic followers, she alone has power to create human life.

---

1. Goleman, *Social Intelligence.*
2. It is outside the brief of this paper to seek to answer whether it is even correct to talk about offending or paining God. We leave others to debate this, but we suggest here that God is somehow deeply grieved by human action, in the way He was with Israel (see Genesis 6:6 ff; 1 Samuel 15:11; Isaiah 63:10).

To woman specifically, aided by man, is given the unique power to create human life. After Adam and Eve, God abdicated this power to create human beings, giving it to man and woman together. But it is woman specifically who is given the power to conceive and create new human life. Would not this arrogant fallen angel, the Enemy of God, also want the male power to impregnate women, creating offspring in *his* evil image? In his hate, the Enemy, much like fallen human nature, would lust for such power. His response could be twofold. One would be to possess men and even women, through which he vicariously procreates, while also wanting to destroy human life. The slaying of women and children has a particularly destructive impact on both individuals and their communities. Many communities in Rwanda have not recovered. Paul Wood comments:

> With the Great Lakes Region being the site of some of the earliest discoveries of human life, and also the source of the River Nile, it is understandable that people like Ugandan Pastor John Mulinde say that the land here has a "birthing" anointing. It is quite feminine in nature. Perhaps that is why there was so much ritual atrocity against women and children. If one is to come through such devastating trauma we have to see beyond it to what God first saw and intended for us. This can give us the hope to struggle through dark days. There is an inheritance worth living for, a prize worth running for. I sense that this region is called to conceive, carry, give birth to, nurture, and release Holy Spirit movements that will impact the whole earth.

Paul Wood continues:

> Yet also, perhaps, like a woman in labor, Rwanda is also so vulnerable and in need of protection while she gives birth. Surely the European colonial Fathers were meant to have done this, but so dreadfully perverted their calling. The

stakes have been raised further by the genocide. The sin has increased, but so has the grace in greater measure. Something incredibly powerful is to be released from this region.

The main feeder of Lake Victoria and the Nile system coming out of Rwanda and Burundi is the Kagera River. It was this river that washed the blood and bodies out of Rwanda and into the Nile Waters. Forty thousand bodies were pulled from the lake and buried in Uganda. About three years ago, while living in Egypt, I had a dream in which I was looking down on the Kagera River where it flowed into Lake Victoria. The Lord simply said, "This is a river of healing."[3]

The Murder of Children

When adults are murdered, they have had some time to live their history and destiny. But taking the life of a child is especially pernicious, removing all hope of their ever writing a history. For the wider human community death also brings to an end all future hope and promise. It erases the possibility of continuing the writing of human history from one generation into the next.

A child is in the image of God in a way that adults are not. Jesus, for example, suggests we must all "become like little children" (Matthew 19:13). So to kill children is to kill something that God particularly values, a certain quality close to his heart. Rwanda had more than its fair share of such genocidal abuse against parents and their children,[4] but in an intergenerational way, this is now being passed on to the children of survivors. AVEGA[5] believes this to be one of the major challenges now facing Rwandan society. They are beginning to observe the

---

3. From personal correspondence.
4. African Rights, "Wounded Generation."
5. AVEGA is a national organization supporting the survivors of the genocide and their dependents.

transmission of trauma across the generations. Because the parents have not been able to resolve all their toxic pain (who is there to show them how?), it is then passed on to the children.[6]

In these comments, we are suggesting that the pain against God can be extended even further. Also, we note from Scripture: "If anyone gives a cup of cold water to one of these little ones, because he is my disciple, he will not lose his reward" (Matthew 10:42). "Come to me all you who are weary and burdened and I will give you rest . . . for I am gentle and humble in heart and you will find rest for your souls" (Matthew 11:28–30). It is therefore easy to deduce that hurting children, the sick, the poor, and the vulnerable further pains God.

God values the qualities of children and calls us all to honor them and bring them to Him. By targeting children for special abuse and destruction, the Enemy achieves maximum damage to human potential, while assaulting God, who loves His created world.

Women as Murderers

Traditionally war is primarily a male pursuit. In biblical times, kings went out to war during the summer season (2 Samuel 11). This remained the case well into the Middle Ages (1500–1600s). The Crusades, for instance, were a summer pursuit for men. But modern warfare is not limited by seasons and includes both men and women in direct combat roles. Although still primarily male, women are now taking a more active part, be it in becoming a female tank commander or pilot, or joining al-Qaeda. To some degree the lines are becoming more and more blurred.

As in most wars, Rwandese men led the way in slaughter. We can almost guarantee that this is what most of our readers will have assumed in reading this book. It is also what is depicted in the films and reports of the genocide. But the reality in 1994 was quite different.

---

6. Rowland-Klein, "The Transmission of Trauma Across Generations: Identification with Parental Trauma in Children of the Holocaust Survivors."

There is disturbing evidence that directly implicates women as murderers. Women participated in killing their neighbors and "friends," and a number are now in prison for genocidal crimes. Most shocking has been the testimonies of women carrying children on their backs while murdering other women as they in turn try to protect their own children. This murderous hate, this addiction, spread to women, too. Quotes the British Medical Journal, "The most horrific massacres occurred in maternity clinics, where people gathered in the belief that no one would kill mothers and new born babies."[7] Women were not merely innocent victims.

As well as the active participation of some, many women are implicated in the murders simply by their silence. We are not blaming women for not getting involved. Many remained silent to stay alive and to keep their children from harm. A religious leader, when speaking to women, asks, "Did you ever pray for the one running for a place to hide? If you did not there is a judgment waiting for you before God. Did you say: 'I am not responsible for my brother'? Or did you pray for those who were being chased?" Many feared for their own lives and the lives of their children, so why would you not want to get involved? Others actively did and were imprisoned. Others died helping their friends.

Another Christian leader asks, "Did you feel badly when your fellow women were raped. Did you put yourself in their shoes? If you did not, if today these men will turn against you—would you enjoy it? Then why did you not do anything?"

What is not yet clear is how directly involved women were in the passion and energy driving the hate in the genocide. It is not known how much the women fed the hate by talking to their husbands, sons, and uncles. But what is known is that overall there was silence from the women. Many women would not have wanted to know what their men

---

7. M. Meredith, The State of Africa: A History of Fifty Years of Independence (London: Free Press, 2005) 515.

were doing. Some perhaps did not know. But did they ask: "Where did you get that meat?" "You had no money, but you bring home looted things." The silence was the betrayal.

Related to this, another aspect of the gender issue is the idea that women themselves are at times best served by removing competition. In Rwandese culture there are more women than men. Also, by far the biggest losers in the genocide were women and children. It is estimated that over 400,000 were infected with HIV/AIDS (in addition to all those who were killed!).

We are not just isolating the role of women in the genocide, for behind the women's behavior was the actions of the men. Even bishops spoke on the radio telling the people to kill Tutsi. As early as the 1950s, Rwandese were taught that killing Tutsi was not a sin because they were "communists," not full citizens. Racial hate was fed.

Bringing Some of These Ideas Together

Bearing traditional Rwandese and Christian values in mind, one begins to see, based on what actually happened, a very complex and multi-faceted stream of events that led up to 1994. From these one hundred days, one grasps the true evil of the genocide in Rwanda and the Great Lakes Region. Much of the killing happened within families. The slaughter was not ethnic. So what have we learned so far?

We see the breakdown of traditional Rwandan society held together by the king and his clan heads. We also see a pernicious, cynical, colonial policy that divided the people through education, so-called religion, and governance. We are also noting that traditional spirituality around the Great Lakes of East Africa may also give us a clue. We are noting that the tribal religions of the region were thought to be more female, and they demanded the human sacrifice of men and boy children to appease them. Children, especially boys, were killed in unprecedented numbers in this genocide. It was also a special feature of the Rwandan genocide that women were targeted and mutilated.

So we are saying that women were specially targeted (with mutilation, HIV/AIDS infection, and other injustices), that children (unusually) were specially targeted, and that men were specially targeted. How is this possible? How can all this have happened and have been reconciled to any sense of love or honor of human life? What we are suggesting is that behind the build-up of the genocidal events is a malevolent evil seeking to fulfill its own pernicious ends regardless of how it might seem to those who were the victims. But we still have one big piece of the puzzle left to note: The shocking compromise of the church in Rwanda.

Group Discussion Questions

1. What do you feel when you hear that women were deliberately infected by men with HIV/AIDS?

2. What is your reaction to the idea of orphans being taken away and treated as slaves?

3. Do you believe a region of bloodshed can become a region of blessing?

4. How do we find a balance between human evil and the role of the Enemy in atrocities like genocide? Who is ultimately responsible?

5. How do we relate the idea of evil to the daily newspaper headlines?

CHAPTER 13

The Role of the Rwandan Church in the Genocide

We have seen that the coming of Christianity to Rwanda did not materially improve many people's lives. Instead of changing their values to what would now be recognized as a Christ-like way, parts of the church fed and exacerbated the hate of Tutsi and Hutu for each other. Despite its emphasis on the family and loving one's neighbors and one's enemies, Christian values were not deeply adopted by all the peoples of this region. Even the amazing intervention of God during the revivals failed to hold on to lasting change. The underlying tensions mounted, and the religious conflict merely added to the divisions. A powder keg was being lit that ultimately led to the beginning of thirty years of genocide.[1]

Blaming God

It is all too easy to blame God for the 1994 genocide. In doing so one misses the point. It is never right to blame God for what one person does to another, even if done in the name of God. There is no worse bigot than a self-righteous one, one who claims God's name to

---

1. Not everyone agrees with our view of a thirty-year genocide. One elder statesman suggested that the genocide began with the arrival of the Europeans in the late 1800s.

justify their own actions and opinions. So one of the tragedies of modern western society is what is sometimes described as the "culture of blame." This is the idea that every time something goes wrong we all have the right to blame someone else. As people, we seem to believe in a simplistic cause and effect: This is what happened, therefore he or she is to blame.

Unfortunately, life is much more complex than that. One thing rarely by itself causes another. Let's say, for instance, that a person catches the flu. We say that the flu virus, therefore, is the reason he is sick. We should also ask why the person got sick. Because of the prevalence of unhealthy lifestyles due to obesity, lack of exercise, and addictions, it is possible that one or more of these contributed to the illness. Thus, catching the flu could be the result of a whole range of neglects in the sick person's life that weakened his immune system. The illness cannot be blamed just on the flu virus.

In the same way, we can all too easily blame God for not stopping the genocide when in reality He had already done much to prevent it: for instance, He intervened in human history through revival and taught the people from Scripture how they should live. Had they lived His values in the way they were called to, they would not have been filled with the racist hate that fed the genocide.

If Rwanda had not been a predominantly Christian country, God would not have been blamed for the genocide. It would be human responsibility. But it is when the church is present that God's name gets tarnished with human action. Where did the church stand during the time of the genocide?

"The Devil Works Best in Wounded Areas"[2]

In the 1959 genocide, the priests and church leaders actively protected the people by allowing them to use the sanctuary of church

---

2. Thank you to Antoine Rutayisire, evangelist, author, and translator, for this helpful concept.

buildings. People were protected. Church leaders allowed people to come into the church compound, and the church leaders defended them. My (Emmanuel's) wife tells me how, at Cyanika in the Kigeme diocese, the missionary took up his gun, shooting into the forest to chase away those coming to kill them. This same missionary also fed those he was protecting. Along similar lines Anglican missionaries took people secretly across the border to safety. King Kigeli's mother, for instance, was taken out of Rwanda by Anglicans when the king was in exile.

In the 1994 genocide, when some of the priests called people to the church for sanctuary, it was sometimes to have them killed. An example of this is the Catholic church of Nyamata, in the Bugesera Region, where in April 1994, in the first few days of the genocide, 10,000 people seeking refuge there were killed in the church buildings and grounds. It is now a genocide memorial site for over 38,000 people killed. A few miles down the road is another genocide memorial site at Ntarama. In other churches, priests were reported to have baptized children because they knew they were about to give them up to be killed.[3]

There were some priests, sisters, and local church leaders who did not protect their Tutsi colleagues, instead handing them over to the militias. Churches were full of Tutsi seeking sanctuary, and many of them died. For instance, Pastor Elizaphan Ntakirutimana received an appeal from two thousand Tutsi rounded up for slaughter in a church. He replied, "There is nothing I can do for you. All you can do is prepare to die, for your time has come."

Also, some of the national leaders were complicit in the slaughter. The Catholic Archbishop Vincent Nsengiyumva, a long-standing ally of the Hutu power movement, quickly offered his support, along with the then Anglican Archbishop Augustin Nshamihigo and some of his bishops (Meredith 2005.513). Summarizes Meredith, "Across Rwanda,

---

3. For this complicity, see T. Salzman, "Catholics & Colonialism: The Church's Failure in Rwanda" (in *High Beam Encyclopedia*, 1997).

church buildings where Tutsi desperately sought sanctuary became the scene of one massacre after another. More people were killed there than anywhere else" (2005.514). Other Christian leaders abetted this slaughter either by omission or commission.[4] The church became the wounder rather than the healer.

Gatwa does a helpful job outlining the role of the church in Rwanda from 1900 through to 1994.[5] The book notes how the church flirted with racial ideology. He suggests that the lack of intervention of the church hierarchy in the 1994 genocide seems to have been an attempt to safeguard the triumph of the "Christian Kingdom in the heart of Africa." He also notes that churches had enormous access to the media, questioning why they failed to create a national conscious- ness of fellowship among Rwandans.[6]

This betrayal has to be balanced by the many unsung heroes who were Christians, believing deeply in their religion of love, service, and courage and seeking to help balance the compromises of their church hierarchies.[7] This included bishops and priests on both sides. For in- stance, the priest of Ruhanga Anglican church, Sostene Renhazo, and his wife, Christine, were killed because he refused to leave his flock. He was a Hutu married to a Tutsi woman. He also refused to give them his wife, so he was killed himself. His church building is now being used as a memorial site because of his bravery and the sacrifice of others.

Division Between Churches

Prior to the beginning of the genocide, the success of the church in Rwanda, especially the Catholic church followed by the Protestant church, was not embraced by everyone in the region. In the 1950s, the

---

4. T. Gatwa, *The Churches and Ethnic Ideology in the Rwandan Crises 1900–1994* (Bletchley, Milton Keynes: Regnum Books, 2005) viii.
5. Gatwa, *Ideology.*
6. Gatwa, *Ideology,* 4.
7. G. Prunier, *The Rwanda Crisis: History of a Genocide* (New York: Columbia Uni- versity Press, 1995) 259.

Belgian vice-governor said he would destroy Catholicism, because he belonged to the Social Party in Belgium—*je vais detruire le cathelisme par les cathelique meme*—"I will destroy Catholicism by using Catholics themselves." He worked with the bishops and missionaries, using the church through its schools and education programs. So not all the guilt for teaching racism can be laid at the feet of the church.

The Belgians also brought the western division between Protestants and Catholics. For instance, the fighting in Uganda, and the dividing of the regions as either Catholic or Anglican, were devised by the Belgians. In these divisions, typically, missionaries never talked to each other, even where they lived in the same city. In Rwanda, Protestant and Catholic missionaries burned each other's churches, and in these towns particularly one now sees the growth of Islam.

What we are suggesting is that relationships have not always been good in these "Christian" regions. Conflict is common and cooperation often absent. For many Rwandese, the combination of this historic conflict and the betrayal of some Christian leaders in the genocide has effectively embittered and disillusioned them. They now look to politics, Islam, or materialism for their faith.

Bishops and Priests

Priests, fathers, and bishops are today on the list of wanted people who would be arrested if they could be found. A number of Christian leaders during the 1980s and 1990s had previously been military chaplains, giving them close connection to the army. When the 1994 genocide started, many of them cooperated with the army. Even Anglican Archbishop Augustine Nshamihigo was implicated and is still on the run. The church accused him and two other bishops of being errand boys for the government. They made a special tour in 1994 to speak to media in Nairobi, Canada, England, and the United States, denying during the genocide that there were any killings. The Rwandan church was corrupt.

Another incident that illustrates this corruption happened to the Dean of the Anglican Cathedral, Canon Karuhije, who was in the church tower and saw murderers coming for him. He managed to get through to a colleague in Canada, who then called Canterbury; Canterbury then called the Dean's bishop, but the bishop ignored the phone call. Two bishops were involved in this betrayal. Some soldiers seized Canon Karuhije from his church and killed him.

One former Anglican archbishop, when the genocide broke out, read from the Psalms on the radio, stating that Tutsi children would become orphaned and Tutsi wives widows. He was cursing the Tutsi and blessing the genocide. Another bishop prayed that the fire from heaven would go to Akagera Park, burning all the Tutsi "cockroaches." This was the region bordering Tanzania where the RPF entered Rwanda. This same bishop said, "The Lord has abandoned you, so don't bother trying to escape." He also visited another part of the country saying, "You are still keeping the [Tutsi] rubbish here. In other places it is clear. It is only here you still keep the rubbish." It is not surprising, therefore, that trust in mainstream Christianity is waning in Rwanda.[8]

Overall, the greatest tragedy of the church was that it was, on the whole, silent. Some suggest politicians politically manipulated this racist behavior, but the evidence suggests that the church often acted on its own in its racist ideology. To its shame, some parts of the church were active both at a national and a local level in promoting the genocide. It both passively and actively became involved in the murder of people. One Christian leader suggested that such racism still exists in the church, but in some denominations more than others. Another leader made the obvious comment that the problem was not so much the racist behavior that followed colonial policy but the silence in not condemning this pernicious ideology.

---

8. Peter and Kibalama (eds.), *Civil Society*, 45.

By not speaking out against the immoral values and hate being promoted by the government and leaders, the church implicitly condoned these values. There is still a need for the church to recover its credibility so that it can play its part in the healing and reconciliation of the country. But this can only be done through the church's confession and repentance of its failures and complicity in the tragedies.[9] But the failure goes well beyond church doors and into the classroom.

The Church as Educator

In bringing Christianity to Rwanda, the church set up mission schools. Over the years the education became a contributor to the genocide, not a bulwark against it. In some ways Christianity illustrated the very worst aspects of education. If the genocide had taken place at the beginning of colonialism the genocide would have been blamed on the "primitive native people." But after one hundred years of "Christian" education, it still happened.[10] In an age of paved roads, international travel, and global telecommunications people seem to have learned very little. Education did not stop the genocide. Both the educated and the illiterate stood together manning the murderous roadblocks. The concern is that what was missing is still missing, that it could happen again. If an educated, civilized society does not help us become more humane, then the value of the education has to be questioned.

Some of the teachers and the educational establishment turned families against each other, especially where there were Hutu-Tutsi mixed marriages. But the educational system also created a Hutu elite, which looked with contempt on all others as illiterate and uneducated. These Hutu-Tutsi formed a political party called *Reder*, a party of the educated who were against their fathers. This was a colonialist strat-

---

9. Gatwa, *Ideology.*
10. It is an interesting question of what the spiritual connection might be between Brussels, center of numerous European blood baths, and Rwanda, one of its protectorates.

egy designed to break down traditional loyalties, especially the family, in order to control the people. *Reder* was the creation of an ethnic elite through education. Across East Africa in the 1920s the Catholic church was urged from Rome to "neglect your churches to build your schools."[11]

The following describes this process. They made schools into a kind of monastery so that the children they took in did not need to go back to their parents. Otherwise, they would get "dirty" again, like washing a pig and then allowing it to go back into the swamp. Taking these children away from their families was a way of saving them from the swamp. But some of the children ran away. In Rwanda, those who went to seminary as teenagers were only allowed to go on holiday once a year.

When the first missionaries arrived in Congo, they handpicked the young attendees of these mission schools. Their residential nature gave the teachers, priests, and nuns considerable control over the children. Separation was at the heart of this type of education, segregation from one's home, family, and community. In effect, it was the breaking down of the family by the church and state.

In my (Emmanuel's) ecclesiology paper, I call the church a center of development but not necessarily a center of the gospel.[12] People pursued education and jobs through the church, but few of them met Jesus. Instead, schools were more centers of progress and opportunity, not places where Christ was formed in them. Education at its best changes the whole person in positive ways. Where education does not do this, it can be guilty of producing an educated oaf, a graduate fool, or even worse, an arrogant self-righteous know-it-all.

---

11. Anderson, *The Church*, 831.
12. E. Kolini, M., *Biblical Ecclesiology* (Alexandria: Virginia Seminary, 1997).

A Biblical Response

It is helpful to note two biblical aspects to this. First, Christ requires that we be like Him, in both our values and lifestyle. He is our lifestyle standard and example, for men and women. Christ placed human life, and especially the sick, elderly, poor, and vulnerable, in a place of special affection. His calling was to them (Luke 4:18–19). But second, one also notes that when a thing like genocide occurs, human worth is ignored and debased. The positive value of human life is no longer a constraint on human behavior. On this basis, any educational system must have at its heart the sanctity and value of all human life, the need to preserve it, and our duty to maintain well being among all people. Any educational system that creates hierarchies, prejudice, or even worse, racism is less than what it should be.

In this sense education at its best must represent the gospel, helping all people who are seeking it to grow into the full stature of their humanity and likeness to Christ. ~~People must learn and live the reality that they are created in God's image. The genocide in Rwanda makes the failure of "Christian" education even more tragic, since it not only failed to stop such slaughter but it also allowed some Christian leaders to be directly involved in the killing~~. Apologies have been expressed, but the wider implications of such failure must still be addressed, especially as they apply to those who were educated in the "church" but are now outside it. Many still carry the legacy of this hate, arrogance, and racism that the misguided system once promoted.

Onlookers see a church that has failed significantly. They also see a church that refuses to apologize because of the legal liability it might incur. The church still needs to admit that it was wrong. The church has a weak theology when it talks about atonement on the one hand but fails to emphasize other values of Scripture, like the values of human life, loving our enemies, and laying aside revenge. Christian education must review its values, but also the church must review what it teaches and how it lives.

Jesus said that He came to look for and save the lost—all who are lost (see Matthew 10:6, 16; 12:11). Our commission is to go to those who are willing to admit their loss. If a person does not admit his lostness, then Christ cannot find him and redeem him. First confessing that one is lost is fundamental to salvation in Christ. We are in danger of seeing, instead, a triumphalist church that preaches gain without preaching human lostness. A true church is a confessing church, a place where truth is spoken in love and forgiveness is lived out.

We, as authors, theologically would argue for promoting a liturgy that highlights values like confession, repentance, and being transparently honest. Repentance is always the work of the Holy Spirit, since there must first be conviction. In teaching a "positive" gospel, we may be in danger of promoting the western-style values of the stiff upper lip, with all its self-control and pretense. We are all tempted to miss or avoid the confession stage because that is the hard part. We quietly say to ourselves that we do not know how to confess, so instead, we put on a mask of forgiveness.

Such an attitude requires that the offended always take the initiative, while the abuser appears to be a disengaged bystander. So there are always two aspects that one should account for, each moving toward the other. Confession becomes easier when both parties come together. Our experience is that the Holy Spirit will always use someone—pastor, counselor, elder—to help us reach confession if we are willing. But then there is also the danger that this is merely one-way forgiveness, talking to someone's back. You cannot keep running after that person. First one must resolve it for one's self.

Also, when looking at failure in the church, we should, ideally, make confession public, although this is not easy. Failure must be brought into the open, because the protection of our society, state, and people is everyone's responsibility, including community and church. The emphasis must move from "small church kingdoms" to the whole community mindset, including the community of the church. For instance, it is everyone's responsibility to care for children, the sick, and the elderly. This is the teaching and heritage of the Old Testament, the New Testament, and the early church. The creation of "little kingdoms" loses the true power of confession, for they allow people to hide. Having presented some of the background to the role of the church in the genocide, let us now look in more detail at how the genocide might have happened.

Group Discussion Questions

1. Do you agree that "the devil works best in wounded areas"? Why or why not?

2. Why did the role of the church so change from the 1959 genocide to the 1994 genocide?

3. What should the position of the Rwandan church have been during the 1994 genocide?

4. What do you think the church in Rwanda should still do to balance its past betrayal of the Lord and the Rwandan people?

5. Do you agree with our emphasis on the need for public confession?

6. Why is public confession so hard for us?

PART FOUR

The Church, Justice, and Healing

We all live in a range of societies. In looking at Africa, we see some societies that are young, still building market economies and the protection of law. Others are far more mature in years with most of these already in place. One type of society does not fit all.

Although controversial, one kind of democracy does not seem to fit all societies either, as we are finding out in places like Afghanistan and Iraq. Some countries seem to thrive more on a strong monarchy type of leadership, while others may even thrive under righteous dictatorships. Whatever type of governance, this book suggests that certain fundamental values are needed in all societies. Without them, we do not have a civilization we all need to live well.

So, what are these fundamentals? Some are moral, like honoring others and what they own. Others are ethical, like discerning what is right and wrong. Others relate to what is culturally acceptable or unacceptable. While other fundamentals relate to the situation as it is at any one time. But for all of us to respond in the right way, we need guidance in what is just, fair, and honoring to others and to ourselves.

People need clear guidance regarding how to respond in the face of a whole range of global and local issues. This is especially true for people who are living in wealthy, well-legislated societies who then want to help in cultures and societies where these do not exist. To make such deep change and establish long-term lasting values takes time—sometimes generations.

But real life is not as simple as that, because not all ideas translate well from one society to another. For instance, in western society there is a strong emphasis on individuality, whereas in traditional African society the emphasis is on what people have in common, what is shared and communally owned. So what can be learned, taught, and transferred, and what would be harmful to a country like Rwanda? And are there values and lessons that Rwanda can teach the rest of the world?

CHAPTER 14

A Therapeutic Response
to the Genocide

*"What cannot be talked about can also not be put to
rest, and if it is not, the wounds continue to fester
from generation to generation."*

—B. Bettelheim[1]

Genocide Survivors and the Healing Journey

Very little work has been done on the impact of genocide on a
whole culture, although a great deal of research has been done on areas like psycho-traumatology, post-traumatic stress disorder (PTSD),[2]
dissociative disorder, and post-torture distress syndrome. Most books
on related subjects do little more than mention genocide.[3] This is not

---

1. B. Bettelheim, "Reflections: Freud and the Soul," *New Yorker* 58 (1982) 52–93.
2. C. R. Brewin, *Posttraumatic Stress Disorder: Malady or Myth?* (New Haven: Yale
University Press, 2003).
3. B. S. N. Goff and K. L. Schwedrdtfeger, "The Systemic Impact of Traumatized
Children," in *Handbook of Stress, Trauma and the Family*, ed. D. R. Catherall (Hove:
Brunner-Routledge, 2004) 179–202; R. H. Klein and V. L. Schermer, "Introduction
and Overview: Creating a Healing Matrix," in *Group Psychotherapy for Psychological
Trauma,* (London: Guilford Press, 2000) 3–46.

because there are not enough genocides to research,[4] but it is probably because some of the more recent ones have occurred in some of the poorest parts of the world, therefore not meriting extensive academic research. The basic damage of abuse and its subsequent trauma in areas like PTSD[5] and dissociative disorders is much better researched.

The findings so far are startling but simple. For a person to achieve release from torture, assault, and major traumatic abuse, it is necessary for them to relive and work through the pain and all the feelings of revenge, ideally within a protective therapeutic setting.[6] It is not the traumatic act as such that usually does the long-term damage to us, though physical harm is normal. Instead it is the toxic traumatic feelings that remain in the body and continue to build over time. They keep the memories alive, though the pain and its trauma will normally lurk just below the surface. A range of avoidant behavioral strategies, sometimes called coping mechanisms, are frequently employed to deny and control this toxic pain.

Symptoms of carrying such long-term trauma include a tendency to loneliness, inability to sustain friendships, a sense of abandonment, recurring loss, powerlessness, depression, and dissolution of the self. The most common symptom is protracted depression, common to almost all clinical studies of chronically traumatized people.[7] But the loss of religious faith is also a symptom: "Never shall I forget those moments which murdered my God and my soul." The loss of faith suf-

---

4. J. Diamond, *The Third Chimpanzee: The Evolution and Future of the Human Animal* (London: Harper Perennial, 1992) 284–286.

5. Royal College of Psychiatrists, *Post-Traumatic Stress Disorder: The Management of PTSD in Adults and Children in Primary and Secondary Care* (London: Gaskell, 2005), National Institute for Clinical Excellence, *Post-Traumatic Stress Disorder: The Management of PTSD in Adults and Children in Primary and Secondary Care*, (Gaskell & British Psychological Society, 2005).

6. A. W. Palachy, "Group Psychotherapy for Victims of Political Torture and Other Forms of Severe Ethnic Persecution," in *Group Psychotherapy for Psychological Trauma*, eds. R. H. Klein and V. L. Schermer (London: Guilford Press, 2000) 265–297.

7. J. L. Herman, *Trauma and Recovery* (London: Pandora, 1997).

fered in chronic trauma merges with the hopelessness of depression.[8] Such trauma does not normally lay hidden. It will on occasions raise its head above the waterline in our lives when it is either disturbed or triggered by circumstances similar to those that caused the trauma in the first place.

Accumulated Pain

We noted earlier in this book the appalling damage that is probably being done in Rwanda by the self-denial of both victims and perpetrators. We often deny the pain in us and do not realize the damage we do to ourselves. What we deny in ourselves still remains accessible to our spiritual Enemy, continuing the abuse of others and ourselves. The pain and its toxic emotion simmer below the surface of our lives. Then suddenly something happens. We see a face that reminds us of someone from the past, or perhaps there is a significant anniversary. Someone may suddenly talk to us about his own memories. All these act as lightening rods of opportunity to trigger buried emotion. Much of the time we will spontaneously dump on others its hurtful toxic contents, while continuing to refuse to deal with the roots or causes.

For instance, many carry the shame of surviving the genocide, yet they have to get on with their lives. Likewise, the trauma of abuse, especially where there is no justice, can fester into a root of bitterness and revenge. This can, in a cancerous way, increasingly sap our energy, while also weakening our immune system. We may also live believing we have survived the worst. ~~Trauma and its subsequent damage will often prevent us from trusting, committing to deep relationship~~s, or ~~being able to share the intimacy of love.~~ No two of us are the same, of course, so we do not all have the same levels of subsequent damage in our lives, even when two of us may have experienced the same thing. There is always much more that is hidden than we realize.

---

8. Herman, *Trauma.*

As a way of coping with such deep personal pain in our lives, we all have a tendency to adjust our lifestyle accordingly, thereby avoiding ever having to face the trauma and its feelings of vulnerability again. One of the tragedies is that we reduce our options in life by saying, for instance, that we will never let a man near us again. Or never trust a woman like her again. We do this out of an instinctive desire to protect ourselves, to reduce the risk of these things ever happening again. But this self-protection actually does the opposite. It prevents us from functioning in anything like a normal healthy manner, making us more vulnerable to ongoing abuse. So we find ourselves with a diminishing range of relationships and options, until we are locked in our darkened room with the curtains closed, refusing to come out.

Some areas of trauma, rage, revenge, guilt, shame, and the like only surface years later. Initially we will go through a period of deep shock and the challenge and stress of accepting what happened. While doing this, we also begin believing we have a future, desiring to reconnect with normal life. So we make plans. Most of these, typically, will not work out, so after a few years we begin to accept the baggage we carry and resign ourselves to the reality that the problems are not going to go away on their own. After ten or more years the problems are still there and often, unbeknown to us, getting steadily worse. But other things are also happening.

Bitterness and its emotion keep the detailed memories alive. The trauma still lurks just below the surface, though we often deny it. We begin to realize we must engage and let go of the pain, or we will be unable to move into our future. For a nation to move into its future, just like individuals, it is first necessary to fully deal with its past. It will not just go away on its own. Emotion, and especially the sense of injustice, will keep the memories just below the surface but as alive as if the trauma only just happened.

Transference

When such deep trauma, pain, anger, and shame are triggered, it will usually result in uncharacteristic outbursts by the victim of abuse. It may be verbal or emotional. It will perhaps appear accidental, disappearing as quickly as it arrived. Very often the outburst by the victim will deeply hurt those around him or her, who often know nothing of the history that has triggered it. To them it feels like an assault. In cultures with such severe buried trauma and abusive ideologies as Rwanda's, retaliating often takes the form of physical, verbal, emotional, and sexual violence.

Many such violent assaults, horrific though they are, are not surprising to a therapist, pastor, or close loved-one. ~~What is happening is called *transference*, the process of a person engaging with his deep toxic historic emotion and then off-loading it on another.~~ Most abuse victims are very guarded about how they carry such toxic pain; they usually will dump it on others only when they are sure that others will not abuse back. No one intentionally picks a fight with a lion! This is why a lot of abuse takes place within the home or against neighbors or others who are more weak or vulnerable than the victim. These people become the lightening rod for all the feelings of anger the abuse victim carries, even though much of the time they are merely the latest in a chain of people who have endured abuse.

In Rwanda at the present time, there are a large number of people carrying such anger, self-hate, and rage. Over a period of years, two things happen. First, the emotion builds and negatively impacts the cellular physical structure of their bodies, which makes matters much worse for them. Over time, this deep emotion becomes increasingly difficult to control, so it spills over and abuses others. In the Rwandan genocide, a second factor was also present: permission to racially hate and harm another.

What we are suggesting, admittedly in a simplistic way, is that one of the basic drives behind the genocide is the racial hatred people carry toward others, built up over many years. It is one of the reasons why the serpent has stayed so strong. A range of toxic feelings will also feed racial hatred. These include jealousy, revenge, fear, self-hate, poverty, and ignorance. The exploding of this rage into physical violence is its transference, and the sacrifice of children is the ultimate form of this rage gone mad.[9]

This toxic racial hatred still lies just below the surface of this nation. We need to draw out this rage within clinical therapeutic environments where it can be transferred in a safe and healthy manner. If we do not do this, then we can only wait for the serpent to again rise above the surface. Until people own their anger, racism, and hate—admitting they carry it, then letting it flood out of them in a healthy way—the threat of it surfacing again must remain.

Forming Healing Support Groups

There are two ways in which the toxic aftermath of trauma will be brought to the surface: randomly, when it is triggered by events, giving many the permission they want to explode into abusive behavior; or deliberately, through healing transference within a therapeutic group, which will contain it and allow the person to renounce it forever.

Within a therapeutic group, one is able to absorb the sin of the hate that people own. If the community is Christian, then they can also be helped in giving it to the Lord. The cross is sufficient. But the group is the agent for this to come to the surface and be discharged. In creating a culture of small support groups across the country, one will see each person go through several stages.

First, trauma victims need the assurance of a safe environment. This will usually take several months. Second, the members of the group, perhaps three to seven in number, need to identify and express

---

9. L. Hirschhorn, "The Modern Project and the Feminisation of Men," in *Organisations, Anxieties, and Defences: Toward a Psychoanalytic Social Psychology*, eds. in R. D. Hinshelwood and M. Chiesa (London: Whurr Publishers, 2002) 35–64.

their anger and rage, admitting what they really feel. Third, the group must support the individual's desire to reintegrate their emotional self, making it possible to live with a future hope, not the despair and pain of their past sicknesses.

This process results in one's calling to the surface all the anger and rage, but instead of a violent transference of it onto others, the group absorbs the pain in a mutual way. We have already noted there is within Rwanda a culture of truth speaking. ~~So we suggest a resurrecting of a Rwandan traditional custom, a restoration of a culture and set of values that would never have allowed the genocide in the first place. Such a healing program becomes a political movement, not modern, not therapeutic, not just Christian, but a value~~ system of support and justice ~~that worked for hundreds of years in Rwanda.~~

This group support model would help diffuse the rage, hate, fear, denial, and dissociative state, allowing people to stop denying that they are suppressing pain. What these hurting people need most is hope that healing docs exist for them—that they can build trust and feel safe enough to be honest with others about their true fears and pain. This is something the culture does not currently promote to the extent that it is needed.

Such a movement would need to grow by replication, by creating and equipping "experts by experience," so that those moving into such a journey, by merely committing to the journey, will begin to benefit immediately. This has got to be a better alternative to deep emotional and physical illness, or to picking up a machete one day, going into an explosive rage, and after the carnage confessing, "I don't know what came over me."

We need to hear Christ tell us it is okay to feel all of our true hate and its pain, owning our racism, woundedness, and self-loathing. For us to harm another, we must first let something die in us. We will have become less than human. Instead, we need to become more fully human by owning, in an honest way, who we have become. So how do we achieve this? One way is through forming therapeutic communities.

Introducing Therapeutic Communities

Therapeutic groups happen when people come together to share in an honest and open way their trauma and toxic pasts. Relationships make us sick, so it must be that relationships bring us healing. The disadvantage of much traditional therapy is that client and therapist often only meet together for several hours a week. The alternative that I (Peter) specialize in is a method where a community agrees together that they want all their relationships, in fact their whole way of life, to be therapeutic. They want to use every opportunity they can to bring healing and wholeness to each other. This is known as a therapeutic community.

There are a number of types of therapeutic communities around the world. Most specialize in one particular area of need, like personality disorder or addictions. The core principles are easily adapted to integrate people with a wide variety of emotional needs. In England, we have been learning how a church can also be a therapeutic community, creating a safe place for people in need. In Belgium there is a whole town that has functioned for hundreds of years as a therapeutic community for people in need.

In a therapeutic community the benefits of a support group are multiplied across every area of daily life, every relationship. Healing and wholeness become integrated into meal times, social events, and general conversation. It can sometimes be a demanding way to live. It requires a high level of openness, trust, and vulnerability. The healing rewards are huge. Its success is related to the level of commitment of all members to support each other in their growing journeys of healing. In many ways, it is not unlike many of the characteristics of the Rwandan revival. More work needs to be done to determine how Rwandan people and survivors of genocide can begin to form therapeutic communities of mutual help and healing with survivors, groups of survivors' children, and convicted killers and their families.

Group Discussion Questions

1. Have you ever had bad experiences that will not go away emotionally?

2. Do you recognize either in yourself or others some of the toxic emotion we are describing?

3. To what extent is toxic emotion responsible for crime and abuse?

4. Was Christ emotional in any way? Did He sin emotionally?

5. How would you feel about adopting a lifestyle where every relationship helped to bring mutual growth and ongoing wholeness?

CHAPTER 15

The Place of Justice

It is not enough to simply offer healing and therapeutic support to those who have been horrifically abused. Scripture is very clear about both the need for reconciliation and the place of justice. Reconciliation is, at its core, a process of transformation for both sides in a conflict.[1]

Justice and reconciliation characterize a healthy society. But we are talking here of a justice that is available not only for those who are powerful, educated, and articulate, but also for those who are oppressed, vulnerable, and poor. Justice must also serve the victim.

The Right for Revenge

Emotion keeps memories alive. A wound has to be exposed, opened, cleansed, treated, and given time before it will heal.[2] Such healing must include the opportunity for justice. It is much harder for people to forgive without knowing and feeling that they have seen justice done against their accusers.

---

1. V. Batts, "Is Reconciliation Possible? Lessons from Combating Modern Racism," in *Waging Reconciliation: God's Mission in a Time of Globalization and Crisis*, ed. I. T. Douglas (New York: Church Publishing Inc., 2002) 38.
2. Gatwa, *The Churches and Ethnic Ideology in the Rwandan Crises 1900–1994* (Bletchley, Milton Keynes: Regnum Books, 2005) 241.

One of the inevitable consequences of unjust slaughter of human life is the subsequent desire of survivors to claim the right of revenge. A biblical interpretation of the law would suggest that everyone has the right to avenge injustice: "an eye for an eye, a tooth for a tooth" (Deuteronomy 19:21). The due process of law must answer injustice with justice. Where this is not completed, people will become disenchanted with the due process of law. The revenge they feel becomes more deeply toxic, and they may take it upon themselves to avenge the wrongdoing if they know the perpetrators.

In a Rwandan setting, justice can be particularly difficult. "No one is in prison for killing the people I loved. I'm the only one that could have put them in prison and I don't even know who they are."[3] Similarly, "I've got nothing to remind me of my parents or brothers. I don't even know where they died."[4] There are many thousands of people who have seen no justice for the appalling losses they experienced.

This lack of justice for so many causes significant problems. We cannot realistically talk about reconciliation and forgiveness unless we have first settled for the survivor the matter of justice and its revenge. One cannot forgive until one has chosen either to pursue justice or has laid down revenge. If justice is not possible, this needs to be acknowledged. There is a separate process that the individual needs to be supported through in order to deal with the emotional consequence of this lack of justice. They must be helped to let go of the anger, the revenge. They must be offered a way of being listened to, being believed, being honored, even when their abuser is unseen and perhaps unknown. Before considering this further, let us look at how Rwandans have recovered the form of justice from their pre-Christian culture, as a response to the genocide.

---

3. African Rights, "Wounded Generation."
4. African Rights, "Wounded Generation."

The Practice of *Gacaca*

Part of Rwandese society under the leadership of the king was the practice of Gacaca. These were people's courts, set up by local Elders, designed to administer reconciliation and justice. Some of these were reinstated after the genocide as a way of bringing genocidaires to trial. Those who planned the crimes and those who deny their guilt are not tried in the Gacaca. But when people are ready to confess and when their crime is limited (they murdered fewer than one hundred people), they are tried locally. For instance, if they were forced into it or were more into looting and personal gain, then the Gacaca was the best place.

The courts are run on three principles. First, the whole village comes together. Everyone attends. They will all know who lived in this village, who died there, and who fled to another place. It is a gathering of the whole community for all to see justice administered and for everyone to have the opportunity to participate. The last few years has seen significant gathering of information on everyone who lived in Rwanda as a result of these community courts.

The next principle is that everyone who comes before the Gacaca court is asked the same questions, "What did you hear at the time of the genocide?" "What did you see?" "What did you do?" Witnesses are called. The community is given the opportunity to speak. It is a place where a person can talk openly and freely, letting go by confessing his anger, revenge, guilt, and pain. These courts can last for several days and are a time of deep emotion.

Another principle of these courts is that they are led by local people of integrity, duly trained. A man may say, "I am a man of integrity," but his son may say, "You are not, you beat your wife," therefore, "You don't qualify!" Seventeen of these people sit together. The Gacaca courts have been running for several years. There are two thousand being held at any one time. They are due to finish their work in 2007, but without helping everyone, by any means.

Many feel that the Gacaca has become a "safe place," a type of confessing church, though the priest is not there to pronounce absolution. Others see Gacaca as a healing clinic. In both cases, confession and justice have traditionally been the role of the church, but it is not being invited to carry this role. When we talk about Gacaca, we are not speaking politically. There is a sense in which God has moved from the church in Rwanda into the Gacaca, because the courts are where the confessing is taking place. We are suggesting that any church that no longer values and practices confession is a dying church.

The Call for Forgiveness and Reconciliation

The tendency in the European and North American church is to emphasize the requirement for forgiveness and even reconciliation, rather than first acknowledge that God is deeply committed to justice. So non-Christians might say, "What do you mean? How can you do that?"

When people try to forgive without having first engaged justice, there is the possibility that they will have an inauthentic repentance. They forgive with their heads but want revenge in their hearts. Many feel "You are telling us to forgive so the abuser gets away without punishment." Much of the genocide was initiated by those in power, by government officials. So people feel as if a representative of their abuser is telling them to forgive, so that the abuser can go free. Rationally, they may know this is not true, but emotionally, transference has occurred and the connections are too strong.

The danger is that society can misunderstand the message of the church to say that victims must forgive *before* they have gone through the just process of settling the right to revenge. This is not true, for it is only after one has dealt with revenge justly that a person can righteously settle the matter by forgiving.

Ideally, justice is administered so that victims can then lay down their revenge and move on into forgiveness. They are free then to recover from their experiences. When justice is not possible, there needs to be alternative ways for victims to be helped to lay down their desire for revenge. Therapeutic support groups can offer an environment, within a trusted small group, for a person to be heard and to let go of his anger and resentment.

Scripture seems to suggest two standards. One is the right for revenge, and the other is the execution of justice for the victim. The idea of justice extends into the teaching of Christ, but here Christ tells us, "Turn the other cheek" (Matthew 5:38), even letting go what is stolen from us. This attitude is further reinforced by the godly attitudes taught in the Beatitudes (Matthew 5:3) and by our Lord's comment that vengeance is His alone (Isaiah 47:3; Jeremiah 50:15).

Christ teaches is that it is not our task as His followers to take upon ourselves the power of revenge. God hears and sees all, and He will avenge the shed blood (John 5:27; Revelation 6:10). Instead, we are required to show love to our enemies and not seek revenge (Luke 6:27). We are not suggesting one surrenders totally the right to due process of law, but the suggestion in the teachings of Christ is that our right to justice should be surrendered to God, while any justice demanded should be tempered by love. So is one looking at two standards?

By laying down the right of revenge and allowing God to be the Avenger, one gives this responsibility to Him. Giving to Christ the right of revenge is a significant benefit to us. This helps us avoid spending a great deal of time and money seeking revenge through the courts. As victimized individuals, we can then get on with our lives rather than remain consumed by all the bitterness and hate for revenge against our perpetrators. But to achieve this we all need to take an emotional journey with Christ, as well as see a restoration of honor of women and children in our culture.

A Call for Greater Honor of Women and Children

The evidence of what happened to women is appalling. But women are beginning to speak out. The problem that interferes most with women "telling all" is that many of the victims and perpetrators are closely related. Women are far more reluctant to accuse men close to them of being genocidaires. Rape victims especially have largely withdrawn from society.[5]

Women may dream of revenge, but the price is often far too high when it so commonly leads to further victimization, local hostility, and segregation. Though they may hate and fear men, many still need the men and the local relationships for their survival. For instance, of the two hundred women interviewed in the 2004 Human Rights report on the present condition of female rape victims, very few had seen justice, and most could not even remember their abusers and so are unlikely to ever see relief.[6] In fact, the courts have sometimes been a forum to further humiliate victims.[7] Justice for such victims is clearly one of the greatest problems.

Speaking out is also very difficult culturally. Within Rwandese society, one does not talk about sexuality in public, though privately, among women-only gatherings, the subject may be addressed. Congregational life can play a key role in encouraging the collecting of such information and taking it to the responsible people. Inevitably, Christian leaders sometimes resist this role out of fear, guilt, and shame. Especially where Christian leaders themselves are not yet absolved of blood guilt, they cannot provide what they do not themselves possess. But the church should make it much easier for women to come forward with evidence. Channels should exist whereby women can give the information to other responsible women, who can then take it forward.

---

5. African Rights, *Broken Bodies*, 67.
6. African Rights, *Broken Bodies*, 76.
7. African Rights, *Broken Bodies*, 82.

One of the problems in Rwanda is convincing women they will be safe if they talk. Also, women need to talk about their toxic pasts, breaking the taboo for their own sakes, for their own emotional health, and for the benefit of others. We are describing the need to create trust. People always ask, "Who am I talking to?" When they try to share painful things with some people, women sometimes hear responses like, "It is nothing more than you deserved." While many others find a sympathizing friend. Learning when it is safe to share is challenging and can have far reaching personal consequences.

The church needs to understand that God has moved out of buildings and into the courts. It should stand with the victims of trauma and offer absolution. In a situation where it is estimated that 60 percent of women who survived death were raped, and 30 percent are now HIV positive, the church has much unfinished business.

The Gacacas are allowing individuals to claim justice and its revenge, creating huge archives. The government is helping women by keeping extensive dossiers on many perpetrators and their victims. Prisoners have also begun to share aspects of their dark past, getting "off their chests" all that they have done. This is very common among inmates. The information available to the government continues to grow through the confessions of convicted genocidals. What many women do not realize is that most of what they might say is probably already known. But until people come forward as witnesses, perpetrators will not be held responsible.

Women need to learn how they can stand up and be a true witness, with a just result. This will be part of their healing journey. But structures need to be strengthened, because not everyone, especially women, feels safe at present.

Could This Ever Happen Again?

We do not believe the 1994 genocide was like a tornado that spent itself and then died. Rather, we see it more like a serpent. It may have gone below the waterline, but it could surface again any time, given the right incentives. This idea contradicts the argument that a country that has experienced such horror will want to ensure that it never happens again. We hear often from those who say it could never happen again, but this belief is not so widely shared as one might assume. The daily reality among many people in Rwanda is the fear that it could happen again. They give several reasons.

First, very few people seem to understand what happened, especially emotionally and spiritually. There is still deep confusion and few explanations. It is far too simplistic to blame it all on racism, the Germans, the Belgians, or the French. Likewise, it is also too simplistic to say it is a Tutsi-Hutu problem.

There is also a clear awareness that not all the leaders of the genocide have been brought to justice. Many are shielded by either the rich or the powerful in Rwanda, in the surrounding countries, or further afield. Some are still protected by the international community who stood by and allowed the genocide to happen. It is quite possible that from exile they are planning both reprisals and a repeat of the genocide that was so meticulously planned while they were in power. In talking with one of the widow groups, these women continue to express deep fear that after they testify in the *Gacaca* they could die the following day. Such fear is not unusual.

Many who participated in the genocide have never been convicted, even though some are well known. Others have served their sentences, been released, and continue to speak openly and without remorse of their ongoing hatred. Added to this is the bizarre situation that even leaders in the church are still in positions of honor and power, despite their being implicated in the genocide. It is little wonder that ordinary people have little confidence in the church.

One of the most disturbing aspects of the current situation seems to be the attitude of many ordinary people who do not trust the country's ability to protect them if they did decide to speak out. At a time when the government leadership is challenging its countrymen to bring forward evidence that will allow for more serious charges, many people continue to hold back. The nation as a whole, and individuals particularly, must be taught how to let go of their past before they are able to move into their futures.

Also the *Gacaca* is a slow process, and some are now saying it does not help. Justice is not being done, they say, so what is the point. In this environment, people decide to keep quiet. Some of the widows are now becoming more desperate and ready to speak out: "I am dead anyway," they say, "killing me would be a favor." Justice has to be one of the tools that will defuse the threat of a further genocide.

Comments Paul Wood, "Regarding the concern of people that this could happen again—genocide is not something the enemy can 'pull out of a hat' any time he wants, or he would surely do so more often. A number of factors and influences have to be brought together at the right time into a critical mass, then a suitable spark to set the whole thing off—in this case an aircraft crash. On the positive side, if only one of the factors can be dealt with, the whole thing will not happen—or will be seriously diminished in scope. The church can work on the few small pieces it has and be encouraged that by doing so it is, like salt, having a significant impact on the health of the nation" (personal correspondence).

The government, led by the president, is seeking to instill in people the belief that they are not Hutu, Tutsi, or Twa, but Rwandese. In order to rebuild the country ideologically, people have got to stop thinking in sectarian ways. This is legislation-driven, but it is also incumbent on all citizens to disclose all they know about the perpetrators of the genocide.

Group Discussion Questions

1. Is it a good thing that learning has been separated from personal positive change?

2. Do we all have the right to expect justice?

3. Is revenge ever wrong?

4. What do we mean by honor for one another?

5. What can the church worldwide do to help Rwanda now?

CHAPTER 16

Launching a Therapeutic Program

Introduction

It has been over a decade since the terrible events of the 1994 genocide, so how do we bring healing to all those who are still alive yet in pain? Large numbers are still traumatized, and the trauma is often severe. This is compounded in that many do not know how sick they really are, because they are not yet admitting that they are not well. They believe they are through the worst, and time will heal what's left.

Helping such people is different from any other traditional clinical or counseling environment. The problem is so big that conventional one-to-one therapeutic processes will never meet the need. Instead, what is required is a movement within the country, led by the Rwandese, that teaches them how to help each other. Those who are in need, those who are taught how to heal themselves with the support of others like them, should build the framework.

We hope you are realizing the immensity of the task. It is a greater challenge than the aftermath of a tsunami, because the true extent of devastation is not yet seen or realized, even by many victims. Also, where there are few answers, people tend to ask fewer questions. It is only when we begin to help a few people that others hear and come along as well. People are willing to admit their need only when they know answers exist that could work for them. In this sense we believe that both the need and the response will mushroom. Only then will we truly begin to see the immensity of the task. But before we look at how to initiate such a program, let us first look at the cost of not doing so.

Compassion Fatigue

There is a cost to caring.[1] For many of us, merely listening about another's traumatic experiences can be traumatizing. Most of us run away from such exposure, not wanting to suffer secondary PTSD. If you consider yourself a rescuer of others, or have deep empathy with the sick or emotionally ill, then you may already be a victim of compassion fatigue.[2]

Compassion fatigue is a secondary emotional illness caused by exposure to those who are in trauma. We noted earlier the role of therapists in the process of transference and the dangers this carries for therapists if they are also not trained to let go of the baggage being dumped on them. Likewise, compassion fatigue is the wearing down process of people's capacity to be continually exposed to other people's abuse, which in turn will take a profound toll on them as helpers. This condition is particularly common among those who have little place to escape such dumping, like people in pastoral ministry, or those who have experienced natural disasters or times of war.

Figley outlines a typical list of compassion fatigue symptoms.[3] These include an inability to make decisions or carry responsibility;

---

1. C. R. Figley, "Compassion Fatigue as a Secondary Traumatic Stress Disorder: An Overview," in *Compassion Fatigue: Coping with Secondary Traumatic Stress Disorder in Those Who Treat the Traumatized*, ed. C. R. Figley (Florence, KY: Brunner Mazel, 1995) 1–20.
2. C. J. Harris, "Sensory-Based Therapy for Crisis Counsellors," in *Compassion Fatigue: Coping with Secondary Traumatic Stress Disorder in Those Who Treat the Traumatized*, ed. C. R. Figley (Florence, KY: Brunner Mazel, 1995) 101–114.
3. Figley, "Compassion Fatigue."

depression; despair; cynicism; alienation from colleagues, friends, and family; job changing; a heavy head; and an attitude that everyone is sick or has problems. If therapists suffer compassion fatigue, they can also traumatize their clients and those around them. Such victims lose their frame of reference, their sense of identity, and their central beliefs and spirituality. The spiritual damage includes loss of meaning, connection, and hope. These can be profoundly destructive. Over time, the personality disintegrates.

It is very likely that a great number of people in Rwanda are suffering various levels of compassion fatigue. Research needs to be done to measure this and then remedial programs started to alleviate the condition. Those most likely to suffer compassion fatigue are family members close to survivors, those seeking to help victims like therapists and pastors, and those in regular contact with traumatized people such as doctors, nurses, and health care professionals. Secondary trauma is very common among therapists who work long term with the traumatized and those who have to live or work alongside those who have experienced trauma.

One antidote is to adopt an "expert by experience" approach to post-trauma needs, where the main therapeutic burden is carried by those who are successfully letting go of their past baggage. They have learned how to be free from the pain and shame of their own pasts. Therefore, they will not be subject to the same danger of "compassion fatigue," unlike their trained but not yet healed professional therapist colleagues. Such experts, by experience, become their own positive message.

The Economic and Political Cost of Ignoring People's Baggage and Pain

Contemporary research has shown beyond reasonable doubt that exposure to traumatic events can produce lasting alterations in the endocrine, autonomic, and central nervous systems. New lines of investigation are showing complex changes in the regulations of stress hormones and in reconfiguring the function and even the structure of specific areas of the brain. For instance, abnormalities have been found in the architecture of the amygdala and the hippocampus, areas that link fear and memory.[4] The political and health care costs in the next decades will be enormous in various parts of the world if programs are not initiated to help alleviate toxic emotion and its long-term psycho-physiological damage.

The long-term impact of trauma on the body, particularly when it is repressed or denied, is now well-established, especially in areas like reduced immunity of the body to disease. Following the threatened nuclear leak at Three Mile Island in March 1979, longitudinal research noted increased levels of cancer and other illnesses as a result of merely the stress of the threat.[5]

Along similar lines, the Iraqi Scud missile attacks on Jerusalem in 1991 had little collateral damage, with only two dead in sixteen days. However, death in the immediate area subsequently rose by 58 percent as a result of the severe emotional trauma caused by the stress and fear of the Iraqi bombardment.[6]

The implications of such findings, when extrapolated, could be extremely serious for many parts of the world where there has been natural or man-made disaster or tragedy. For instance, a twenty-year study in the US noted that depressed people are twice as likely to develop a fatal cancer in the years ahead, and they are far more prone to addictive disorders.[7] The physical conditions are absolutely real, diagnosable, and sometimes treatable, but the roots and drivers are often emotional.

If nothing is done, over the next decade the Rwandan government will need to spend far more money on health care, as well as

---

4. Herman, *Trauma*.
5. P. Martin, *The Sickening Mind: Brain, Behaviour, Immunity, Disease* (London: Flamingo, 1998).
6. Martin, *Sickening Mind*.
7. Martin, *Sickening Mind*, 96–97.

calculate the cost of losing increasing numbers of people prematurely. Consequently, the mental and emotional damage will continue to worsen for survivors who have witnessed the loss of their loved ones. A doctor working with one of the aid programs said that we are just now beginning to see the physical, emotional, and spiritual damage done to individuals and the whole nation.

Not only women and children, but men are also beginning to show a range of psycho-physiological illnesses that were uncommon in the past. The self-denial and repression of deep pain and trauma by tens of thousands of people will inevitably express itself, surfacing in a range of ways such as ulcers, cancers, heart disease, physical pain, and other disorders. One wonders what many genocidaires now feel about what they have done: the guilt, fear, shame, and pain of their actions. How will their toxic pasts affect them physically? Such men and women may need to be offered some kind of amnesty in order for them to come forward and settle matters with both their Maker and their victims.

One further dimension must also be brought into the equation. As Rwandan society becomes wealthier and imports western lifestyles like smoking cigarettes, using drugs, drinking alcohol, and having casual, unprotected sex, related diseases will emerge. These added to existing emotional disorders create problems unprecedented in any culture at any time. We have an endemic problem waiting to explode, for when people who are already carrying pain and trauma are given the opportunity to further abuse themselves in a socially acceptable way, some always will in a big way.

A Network of Support Groups Across the Country

In suggesting a network of support groups across the country facilitated by those learning to heal, "experts by experience," we are entering new territory for many. Within these groups recovery unfolds in three stages: first by establishing safety, followed by remembering

~~and mourning,~~ then by reconnecting with ordinary life.[8] The support ~~group creates a safe place and overcomes walls of shame and~~ chosen ~~willful incapacity to link and relate with a person~~'s past.

It also opens a space for the traumatized to share and emotionally engage this trauma, to work through all the deficiencies of self-esteem, breaking self-accusations and all the insecurities that go with it. Such groups need to be heterogenous, not comprised of trauma victims alone. The group becomes a container of unbearable feelings, allowing the whole group to absorb what any one person would find very difficult to carry.

Within the church, we will bring a person to the cross for forgiveness of sins. This can be a life-changing moment. What we often do not do is also teach them to experience an emotional engaging of all of their racial hate that lies just below the waterline of their conscious lives. Confession in the church in Rwanda must include not only what we have done (both our sin and our thoughts) but also what others have taught us wrongly or done to us that we now need to surrender emotionally to the Lord. Of course, this does not apply just to Rwanda. Around the world the church would benefit from introducing this deeper level of cleansing to those who are coming to Christ.

We need to create a culture, both emotionally and relationally, where Christ not only takes our sin but also our shameful hate, racism, and pain. One has to create an environment where it is safe for people to express what they are feeling. In such a group of equals, with a facilitator, they will be able to confess and speak out what they really feel.

Many people in Rwanda are currently afraid to do this for a number of reasons both cultural and personal. Sharing any form of weakness is not always advisable in the Rwandese culture. Another problem is that once people admit what they really feel, they then have a duty to themselves to do something about it. Because they do not have this

---

8. Herman, *Trauma*.

opportunity, they remain in denial. We are often taught to forgive, but currently Rwandese are not being taught that Christ says it's okay to feel anger, it's okay to feel revenge, it's okay to want justice, and it's okay to feel loss. It is healing to share pain with Christ and others. But other problems stand in the path to any significant numbers of Rwandese embarking on such a journey.

Creating Safe Places

One of the needs often mentioned to us is the lack of safe places where women in particular are able to relax, feel at ease, and begin to share their horror. Most women are part of extended families, all living together, often with a number of people in the same room. Many of these people have their own toxic pasts to contend with. So the need for a safe place is central to any therapeutic initiative.

What is also needed is to find Rwandese willing to take a healing journey themselves and then to support other men and women in their desire to be emotionally free from their pasts. Creating safe places is just the first step, because such a healing movement will take hold only if people themselves begin to possess and live out the healing they are being offered. They must become "experts by experience" in first helping themselves; then they must be willing to help others.

A Movement of "Experts by Experience"

The client ultimately makes the best expert. We need to create a movement of people possessing their healing who are then willing and able to help others. To do this we should use existing social networks along with new initiatives to build therapeutic relational healing into a culture of friendships. We must create and affirm a generation of "experts by experience" who can then be accredited professionally, allowing them to become trainers and facilitators for further groups. This will begin to create across Rwanda what is called a "healing matrix,"[9] where both intellectual healing and emotional release can be practiced.[10] Such a strategy will lead to further networks of support for those seeking help.

How to Start

The last one hundred years in Rwanda have seen an enormous breakdown in trust. The colonials promoted division between Tutsi and Hutu, destroying relational society and its traditional structures. People lost or had stolen from them their long-held values. Many were taught to be suspicious of family life and its worth. They were taught that their first loyalty must be to the church. Education in a "Christian" school could demand a level of loyalty from both leaders and clergy that undermined more traditional family structures. Also, from the 1960s onward, such suspicion grew within both Hutu and Tutsi families and communities.

We worry that for a relational, therapeutic program to be learned, people need to become more open, even to appreciate and believe in the benefits of telling the truth within a group they can trust. "I don't want to tell them my problems" is commonly heard. So how will people trust each other? Ideally, relationships of trust that already exist can be used for building therapeutic groups.

One should be cautious in adopting such groups. Therapeutic groups will never work where there are hierarchies, where one person is the boss and the others are followers. Therapeutic groups also need to meet in neutral places where everyone can feel safe. Such centers need

---

9. R. H. Klein and V. L. Schermer, *Group Psychotherapy for Psychological Trauma* (London: Guilford Press, 2000).

10.   E. Hegeman and A. Wohl, "Management of Trauma-Related Affect, Defences and Dissociative States," in *Group Psychotherapy for Psychological Trauma*, eds. R. H. Klein and V. L. Schermer (London: Guilford Press, 2000) 64–88.

to be established all over the country, running workshops and support groups. We are sure that Rwandese will quickly learn, in a climate of mutuality, how to become "experts by experience."

Setting up such networks will also release a movement of lay people able to share with others their own initial healing, thereby replicating themselves throughout the country. This movement should be independent and led by Rwandese. Those who emerge as leaders can also be accredited professionally, vocationally, and academically.

Group Discussion Questions

1. Can you conceive of people having no place to go that is safe for them?

2. What would be the difference between your discipleship group and a therapeutic support group?

3. How would you seek to restore trust among people?

4. Do you agree with the suggestion that our emotional life can contribute to our becoming physically ill?

5. Do you know anyone suffering from compassion fatigue?

6. Note some of the ways we can prevent racism in our culture.

7. Do you agree with the idea that many people will not admit a problem or need until they know someone has a solution?

PART FIVE

An Action Plan

Most case studies end with a conclusion, a statement of the findings, and a suggestion on whether the outcomes are applicable to other contexts. In a situation of such human tragedy as Rwanda, we do not aspire to this kind of dispassionate response. Instead, we have viewed this book more in line with an action-research model that seeks to suggest interventions, resulting from the research that may help resolve or ease the deeper problem.

In Rwanda, the problems are vast. The poverty, the lack of infrastructure, the loss of leadership, the number of orphans and widows, the pain and trauma—these are taking many years of committed support to resolve. In this book, we have focused just on one—the need to understand how the genocide occurred in order to minimize the possibility of its recurrence and maximize the potential for healing.

So in this final part we will explore some possible areas of response. Many of these ideas are directly applicable to other situations where there has been terrible tragedy, for instance, those displaced or left behind after Hurricane Katrina, the thousands of homeless in Pakistan after the earthquakes, or those indelibly scarred from the trauma of the 2005 tsunami. Some of what we suggest here will have obvious relevance. Another example would be war-torn countries and those where genocide or democide are being practiced even now, such as Iraq, Afghanistan, and Sudan.

It is also our hope that some of the ideas suggested will also be directly relevant to our readers, that some will be implemented in your own local community where people are feeling abused, disadvantaged, or voiceless. However, our primary goal is to propose a way forward to support the people of Rwanda. Also, we are proposing an action plan for the church, both in Rwanda and internationally. There are, of course, more ideas than we have suggested. This is just a start—important ways that Christ can walk again in lands and lives where His love has been lost or never known.

CHAPTER 17

Outlining a Way Forward for Rwanda

"Rwanda Help Heal Yourself"

The following is nothing more than a "shopping list" of some of the things that need to be taken into account in any future strategy to help Rwanda heal itself. Most of the ideas are not new; they do not claim to be. The two lists in these chapters for society and the church are merely intended as reminders of all that you have read and now could apply if you so wished. Together all of our efforts could form a basis to help heal Rwanda, along with others not mentioned.

A Life Full of Loss

Rwanda has yet to fully own the true extent of its losses. All boundary violations, in any form, create loss. Both society and the church in Rwanda need to begin writing a social psychology of loss and how they might redeem it in their lives.[1] Groups lend a kind of formality and ritual solemnity to individual grief; they help survivors pay homage to

---

1. A. Matsakis, "Trauma and Its Impact on Families," in *Handbook of Stress, Trauma, and the Family*, ed. D.R. Catherall (New York: Brunner Routledge, 2004) 15–32.

their losses in the past while repopulating lives in the present.[2] This loss cannot be redeemed unless it is first fully owned, and this will require teaching and learning.

The Scourge of Emotional and Physical Illness

We have to take serious account of psychophysiology, the long-term negative impact of toxic emotion on the human body. We must also measure the impact of psycho-neural immunology, the damage done by toxic emotion to the nervous and immune systems of the body, weakening its capacity to resist illness. People must find safe places where they can openly "fall apart" on the path to greater wholeness.[3] Few such places currently exist, especially for women. AVEGA suggests such issues need to be tackled as part of a major holistic program for the thousands of women caught in this trap. Such support must include safe houses, rehousing, trauma relief, medical support, and justice against abusers. But we should not restrict this to survivors, since we also need to take seriously the children of those who carry trauma.

Intergenerational Transmission of Trauma

Based on holocaust survivors, long-term research is demonstrating that the children of survivors can often have more serious symptoms of the trauma than their parents.[4] Much research confirming this fact has already been done in this area.[5] Extending the heavy cost to our children[6] is profoundly disturbing if we do not diffuse it now in the

---

2. Herman, *Trauma*.
3. Hegeman and Wohl, "Management."
4. Rowland-Klein, "Trauma."
5. B. S. N. Goff and K. L. Schwedrdtfeger, "The Systemic Impact of Traumatized Children" in *Handbook of Stress, Trauma, and the Family*, ed. D. R. Catherall (Hove: Brunner-Routledge, 2004) 179–202.
6. T. Kaplan, "Psychological Responses to Interpersonal Violence: Children," in *Psychological Trauma: A Developmental Approach*, eds. D. Black, et al. (London: Gaskell, 1997) 184–198.

parents. Tackling the intergenerational aspect of the trauma will naturally break the cycle of damage in the next. Breaking such violence will not be easy.

Breaking the Cycle of Violence

Strong evidence now exists that the abused can become the abuser.[7] Mandela notes this in his report on violence in the twentieth century. The church must begin to allow people to own their anger, rage, and pain, teaching them that the cross is able to absorb all they wish to own in themselves. They can, without shame, give it to Christ in the witness of others. As Dennis Martin so ably suggested in the 1960s, the church has a duty to absorb such evil, but in many ways it is currently far too controlled and respectable to take on the messy and risky task of mitigating human pain and disorder.[8] All of us are vulnerable to the abuse of the baggage of those we seek to help, especially if we are healers ourselves.

Begin Healing the Healers

We must begin to account for compassion fatigue[9] and build into the infrastructure of society workshops and retreats that allow therapeutic support workers to off-load the baggage that has been dumped on them by others. We must begin to help heal the healers. A traditional society that exercises justice will also reduce the power to abuse, and some of these values need to be recovered.

---

7. G. Mezey, "Psychological Responses to Interpersonal Violence: Adults," in *Psychological Trauma: A Developmental Approach* eds. D. Black, et al. (London: Gaskell, 1997) 176–183.

8. D. V. Martin, *Adventure in Psychiatry: Social Change in a Mental Hospital* (London: Bruno Cassirer Publications, 1962) 185.

9. L. A. Pearlman and K. W. Saakvitne, "Treating Therapists with Vicarious Traumatization and Secondary Traumatic Stress Disorder," in *Compassion Fatigue: Coping with Secondary Traumatic Stress Disorder in Those Who Treat the Traumatized,* ed. C. R. Figley,(Florence, KY: Brunner Mazel, 1995) 150–177.

Restoring Traditional Rwandan Values

We must begin to restore respect for a range of traditional Rwandan values, like a greater respect for the elderly, the "gray hairs," and a greater sense of national cohesion and unity. We should allow for the pride of integrity to be restored to Rwandan identity. Some of these values are trust, honesty, and openness.

Trust, Honesty, and Openness

Abusive damage in our lives removes much of our ability to trust relationships with others. We must give people a reason to trust again, restoring a willingness to talk with one another and to trust those who help them and walk the road with them. Restoring a traditional story-telling culture and its values would help achieve this, since trust, honesty, and openness will follow thereby contributing to Rwanda becoming a safe place for safe people.

Creating Safe Places and Safe People

Trauma and emotional illness separate people,[10] so it is essential that we begin building more safe places and safe people who can help support those seeking positive change in their lives. Together, in support groups for both men and women, we constitute the norm from which we deviate individually.[11] Such support groups will help reduce PTSD symptoms as well as teach, tell, and witness to past trauma. Safe places and safe people allow for grieving, help restructure people's lives, restore them to reality, and help reintegrate them into society.[12] This will allow people to become "experts by experience." In creating safe places we must also help teach people to be safe, especially the abusers, so they do not want to abuse again.

---

10. Herman, *Trauma*.
11. Klein and Schermer, "Introduction."
12. Klein and Schermer, "Introduction."

Helping the Abusers

In the western world, it has been necessary to turn some prisons into therapeutic communities,[13] since a two-year therapeutic program will bring down reoffending rates significantly.[14] ~~While initiating a program for the abused, we believe it is also important to begin programs for convicted genocidaires.~~ We recommend turning some prisons into therapeutic communities that can help abusers see more clearly what they have done, help them understand why the genocide happened, and teach them to begin a journey of exploring new values that will help them avoid ever wanting to hurt others again. The benefits could be incalculable, especially in helping defuse racial hate or abusive intent the convicted person may still carry. But education must also play its part.

Values-Based Education

Because education was part of the genocide story, educators now have a fundamental duty to enable and empower future generations. Values-based approaches to education policy and practice positively impact how all of us learn and behave. A range of core values must be embraced as a foundation of education in Rwanda and embedded in policy, practices, and guidance frameworks. Values should touch every aspect of managing and learning in a school. Values-based education by definition and practice places the child at its heart. As with good parenting, it builds self-belief, self-efficacy, and personal responsibility. Many of Rwanda's young learners have been denied traditional parenting; educators therefore have a role to play *in loco parentis.* A national values-based approach to Rwanda's educational policy and practice

---

13.   <http://www.psyctc.org/iafp/nl_3_1/grendon.html>. For an introduction to prison therapeutic communities, see Parker (2006).
14.   <www.homeoffice.gov.uk/rds/pdfs/r53.pdf>.

would provide a positive foundation for personal and national growth toward maturity.

Group Discussion Questions

1. Do you agree that a matter can only be fully redeemed after it has been fully owned?

2. Does it concern you that one's unresolved issues will be passed on to the next generation?

3. What is more important, safe places or safe people?

4. How do you respond to the idea of people who are successfully taking a therapeutic journey being called "experts by experience"?

5. Is the role of the church and that of the therapist distinct, or should they be the same?

CHAPTER 18

How Can the Church Respond?

"We must empty ourselves, therefore, of the immoder-
ately high faith we have in ourselves . . [since] nothing
good can come from us. And should, by chance, an un-
selfish thought arise . . . you may be sure that it does not
come from you, but is scooped up from the wellspring
of goodness and bestowed upon you: it is a gift from
the Giver of life. Similarly the power to put the good
thoughts into practice is not your own, but is given you
by the Holy Spirit."

—Tito Colliander[1]

We have described in this book a country that feels that God was
lost at the time of the 1994 genocide. So today, much of the church's
mission is to find ways of helping God be rediscovered. We are not pre-
tending this is an easy task. Betrayal in any form leaves lasting damage
in us. We then have to be given good reasons to trust and love again.

---

1. T. Colliander, "On the Insufficiency of Human Strength," in *Way of the Ascetics:*
The Ancient Tradition of Discipline and Inner Growth, ed. T. Colliander (New York:
St. Vladimirs Press, 1985).

With God's help, we believe this national problem can be reversed. What follows are some of the ways we can all help achieve this.

Restoring Confidence in the Church

Paul Wood responds: "Authoritarian structures have failed in the past, and they may yet hinder a generation of young people who can see the way forward and who are called to take the lead in the next stage of the race. The future hope lies with the young generation—the very ones the genocide sought to eliminate. Can the Rwandan church dismantle the authoritarian control of the previous generations and serve the rising generation? Can any church do that?" One of the ways we can help this confidence be restored is if we are willing to teach people how to deal with their loss.

Writing a Theology of Loss

Loss is one of the greatest areas of pain in the Rwandese people's lives. But few of us, either inside or outside the church, have the teaching or experience in how to deal with loss, even though many passages of Scripture talk about loss of life, limb, loved ones, job, home, future hope, and even relationship with God. A theology of loss in a Rwandan setting has to be one of the greatest current needs in the church. For many, God has been part of the problem, so it is important that He now be part of the solution.

God Is Part of the Answer

In both material reality and in the spiritual landscape there is an offense being committed every time human blood is shed. There is an addictive attraction for some in having the power to do evil, especially when one is given permission to do so, as in democide. In one sense we are all involved in such atrocities, either through a naive innocence or duplicity. We become what we do, and doing nothing is sometimes as bad as willfully doing harm. So as human beings we have all been part of this tragedy, but we are now able to respond in a positive way by learning to do what we can. ~~God was not in the genocide as an instigator in any way. Like us, He can be part of the solution. But first we must learn to apologize.~~

Apologizing

~~We need to apologize to the Lord for the disgraceful behavior of people's atrocities against one another, especially when those perpetrators were in the church.~~ We should also note the part of western governments and the western church in not doing more. Also, we should not forget our own part, our chosen indifference to what has happened. Where were you in June 1994? We should all approach this part of the world with an apology. Unless we come in humility of spirit we will not be able to serve in the ways we need to. But our apologies are merely a precursor to the really deep need we have to find our tears. One of the key ways we say we're sorry is through our tears.

Rwanda, Find Your Tears

Women are allowed to cry, to shed tears, but men are not. Women are allowed to express their emotion, but men are not because men are fighters and soldiers and they are not meant to express their feelings. They have to be tough. This is part of Rwandan culture and training. "My tears were beaten out of me, my family used to hit me until I stopped crying." What we deny in ourselves becomes the groundwork for a range of long-term illnesses that add to the pain of the historic abuse. ~~A wave of tears must begin with the leaders, as examples to the nation.~~ Many leaders told us they are as sick as everyone else. So let us lead with our tears. And in this way we will all be able to begin practicing renouncing what happened and seek to change it.

The Church Renouncing the Genocide

There is a specific need for the church in Rwanda, and for the international community, to renounce the genocide and commit to create safe places, both as a response to hurting people and for future generations. The church has to say "never again" and possibly through a Charter articulate the values of the new society that is being sought by many. Then it must commit to living this Charter in all areas of influence. Confession should be part of the ministry of the church, bringing truth to the surface.

Bringing Truth to the Surface

In apologizing, we must also choose to lay at the foot of the cross our right for and desire for revenge. As Golda Meir once suggested, there will be no peace until we love our children more than we want revenge. In doing this we also need to invite the Holy Spirit to do what He does best: bring the truth of what happened to the surface, where individuals and the nation of Rwanda can deal with it justly and finally. People need to feel safe before they will be willing to speak out. The truth has still to be told by many who have not yet spoken out. The truth must be brought to the surface. Fear must give way to a sense of sharing what is true so it can be acted on here and now. Such a way forward will expose the Enemy and people's allegiance with his values.

The Enemy of Truth and God

People's baggage and trauma, with all their secrets and fears, hold them back from doing what is right. It is always so much easier to deny what happened than to let the truth engage and flood you. One's unrighteous hate is fed by the Enemy of God. Justice is denied to those who most need it. There must be a movement in the Great Lakes Region that will begin to believe we can claim our own destiny, welcoming truth and bringing to the surface all that is still hidden. In this way, we can begin to redeem all that has been lost to the Lord and to us.

Redeeming Spiritual Losses

In Rwanda, we have witnessed the loss of a generation of gifting and spiritual anointing. It is very important for the survival of the church in Rwanda, and indeed the survival of the Rwandan culture, that we do not allow this spiritual gifting and anointing to be lost to the nation or the church for future generations. We must invite the Lord to give it back in both the very young and the youth so that future generations will begin to redeem what has been stolen and temporarily lost. For this we need a church that stops being passive and takes action.

Bringing an End to Passivity

For redemption to happen there must be an end to passivity, especially among women and young people. We need to find ways to birth an empowering movement that gives people safe places to begin to speak the truth of what happened to them and their families. Some people will need to be taught how to speak up, beginning to believe their opinion is significant. In this way, they can let go of guilt and shame.

Letting Go of Guilt and Shame

Many are living under the shame of what happened, and they need to be given permission to leave it behind. Not leaving the shame as dissociation, however, but by engaging the trauma and pain of what happened and beginning to be free from their pasts. In doing so they will learn how they can embrace life again. Our hearts must contribute to changing this nation so that enough people will let go of their rage, giving it to Christ within support groups and so diffuse the bomb. For it is only when people feel safe that they are able to speak out and help others.

Helping People Feel Safe

There is a deep need for people to feel safe in Rwanda. Are they really free from their enemies? If they speak up will they be punished, or can they ask for help? Who should they ask? Some are questioning, "Will Rwanda ever feel safe?" The churches have a crucial role in providing a container for all this fear, anger, frustration, and suffering, thereby exposing evil.[2] As people feel safe they can begin being reconciled to themselves, to others, and to God.

Reconciliation

There is a great need for reconciliation.[3] Until enemies are willing to apologize to each other and let themselves be reconciled, little can be achieved with so many broken families and relationships. Acknowledging the right to justice must precede all reconciliation. This must be settled first. Then and only then can true reconciliation be found. And reconciliation is the next step to healing and wholeness.

Beyond Reconciliation to Healing and Wholeness

We have a nation of "spiritual refugees" because of the genocide. Many people do not know their parents or how old they themselves are. So many villages were destroyed that people are growing up without a personal history. We need to write a theology of "Father God," the Family of God with a hope of restoration. Christ as Healer and Restorer must be given His place in the church in a way that He has never before been given. This will help heal people so they will be able to walk where darkness dwelt.

---

2. Gatwa, *Ideology*, 255.

3. For a Rwandan comment on the problem of reconciliation, see C. P. Sarfari, "Challenge to Reconciliation in Rwanda Following the 1994 Genocide: Theological Perspectives," (2006, online), <http://www.theo.kuleaven.be/page/doctoraltheses/107/> (accessed April 15, 2006).

Prayer Walking

We need to begin to criss-cross the country, prayer walking with the light of Christ and our feet shod with the gospel of redemption and healing, not just of salvation. We must engage in prayer walking that redeems the land that was stolen by the appalling bloodshed. Pray that the country will be sacred to Christ and that the Rwandan people will welcome His healing presence. We should especially address the idea of the curse of the shed blood in the soil.

Group Discussion Questions

1. What do we mean by saying God should be part of the solution, no longer part of the problem?

2. Why do people find it so difficult to show their tears?

3. Do you agree with Golda Meir that there will be no peace until we love our children more than revenge?

4. Most of us are fearful to commit to deep change in our lives. Why is this often the case?

5. Do you agree that the church has a responsibility to confront evil?

Conclusion

The protracted genocide discussed and illustrated in this book was not the work of a mysterious Enemy. Instead, it was the intentional tragic consequence of a deliberate ideology of racism and hate, an ideology reinforced through government, the church, and education. Behind it, hidden, was the opportunistic intent of the Enemy. The goal was the systematic extermination of a people defined artificially by appearance and fortune.

In this book, we have noted two distinct and related messages. The first is one of healing and wholeness from our pasts. Christianity has for hundreds of years preached a gospel of salvation to Africa, on the whole successfully. But for some parts of Africa today we must preach the *whole* gospel. Salvation is indeed part of this process, but personal and relational transformation must also be part of the gospel message. The biblical concept of *shalom* (peace) for all mankind speaks of every aspect of salvation: past, present, and future.[1]

One key gift of this *shalom* is our personal and relational healing, our possessing a wholeness that we can get in no other way. Christ takes our pain and leads us into a way of life where we can let go of our pasts and be free from their toxic trauma. By doing this we become more hu-

---

1. Thank you to Michael Green for this idea. E. M. B. Green, *The Meaning of Salvation* (London: Hodder & Stoughton, 1965).

man, more mature, more whole, and a lot more competent in valuing other people and relationships.[2] Healing from our pasts is a fundamental part of being transformed in Christ.[3] Through this *shalom*, Christ has not called us to manage our pain, but to genuinely give it to Him so we can be free from it.

The second message of this book is just as radical. We have noted that the serpent still lurks just below the surface, surfacing again and again with its genocidal ideology. A firm response to this serious threat, therefore, needs to occur in two stages. First we need strong leadership—government and church—that like the kings of old, can say no and enforce it, when and where necessary. While this firm hand holds extremism in check, in any form, we should also be passionately teaching the next generation new values in citizenship, moral integrity, and the value of all human life.

In the short term, we would rather see very firm leaders who can hold the middle ground keeping peace across the nation while the process of nurturing democracy grows stronger and stronger. Democracy in Europe took hundreds of years to evolve. It is a learning journey. Realistically, our true hope for both this nation and the whole region is in our children and their children.

Therefore, what we are saying is that saving life in the short term is more important than achieving a superficial democratic process that is unable to maintain consistent ongoing peace. The maintenance of peace must continue to be achieved, even where it may take the form of a righteous fear of governance in the short term. The serpent must not be allowed to rise again. It must be starved of its racist hate and power.

May God help us.

May God help heal Rwanda.

---

2. P. R. Holmes and S. B. Williams, *Church as a Safe Place: A Handbook. Confronting, Resolving and Minimising Abuse in the Church* (Bletchley: Authentic, 2007).
3. P. R. Holmes and S. B. Williams, *Becoming More Like Christ: Introducing a Biblical Contemporary Journey* (Milton Keynes: Paternoster, 2007).

RWANDA:
HOW YOU CAN HELP

LIFE GIVING TRUST: www.lifegivingtrust.org

Prayer

Prayer is desperately needed for the survival and prospering of the Church in East Africa and around the world. For an update of all these needs see our website, www.lifegivingtrust.org.

Giving a Financial Gift

A little money goes a long way in helping needy people. If you are able to make a financial gift, so that we can offer support and training to more people, we and they would be very grateful. Have a look at our website for several easy ways to give, www.lifegivingtrust.org.

Supporting a Specific Project

We have a range of projects that you can support. These include sponsoring workshops, supporting a trauma center, financing a vehicle, etc. For more details visit our website, www.lifegivingtrust.org.

Our Ministry of Reconciliation

Both authors are on the frontline of reconciliation and wholeness ministry. If you wish to support this work, or either of the authors in his ministry, you can do so by contacting them through the website, www.lifegivingtrust.org.

Other Books by
Dr. Peter R. Holmes

Letting God Heal: From Emotional Illness to Wholeness, co-authored with S. B. Williams, (Authentic, 2004).

Becoming More Human: Exploring the Interface of Spirituality, Discipleship and Therapeutic Faith Community, (Paternoster, 2005).

Changed Lives: Extraordinary Stories of Ordinary People, co-authored with S. B. Williams, (Authentic, 2005).

Becoming More Like Christ: Introducing a Biblical Contemporary Journey, co-authored with S. B. Williams, (Paternoster, 2007).

Trinity in Human Community: Exploring Congregational Life in the Image of the Social Trinity, (Paternoster, 2007).

Church as a Safe Place: A Handbook. Confronting, Resolving and Minimizing Abuse in the Church, co-authored with S. B. Williams, (Authentic, 2008).

Fasting: A Biblical Handbook, (Paternoster, 2008).

"Some of the Problems of Studying Spirituality," in Flanagan, K. and Jupp, P., *Sociology of Spirituality,* (Ashgate, 2008).

Bibliography

African Rights. *Rwanda: Death, Despair and Defiance*. London: African Rights, 1995.

——. *Left to Die: At ETO and Nyanza: The Stories of Rwandese Civilians Abandoned by UN Troops on April 11, 1994*. London & Kigali: African Rights, 2001.

——. *Rwanda: Broken Bodies, Torn Spirits. Living with Genocide, Rape, and HIV/AIDS*. Kigali: 2004.

——. "A Wounded Generation: The Children Who Survived Rwanda's Genocide." African Rights. <www.africanrights. org>.

Allen, T. "Understanding Alice: Uganda's Holy Spirit Movement in Context." *Africa* 61 (1991): 3ff.

Anderson, W. B. *The Church in East Africa 1840–1974*. Dodoma: Central Tanganyika Press, 1977.

Ashford, M. W. and G. Dauncey. *Enough Blood Shed: 101 Solutions to Violence, Terror and War*. New Society Publishers, 2005.

Batts, V. "Is Reconciliation Possible? Lessons from Combating Modern Racism." In *Waging Reconciliation: God's Mission in a Time of Globalization and Crisis*, edited by I. T. Douglas, 23–49. New York: Church Publishing Inc., 2002.

Bettelheim, B. "Reflections: Freud and the Soul." *New Yorker* 58 (1982): 52–93.

Bilinda, L. *With What Remains: A Widow's Quest for Truth in Rwanda.* London: Hodder & Stoughton, 2006.

Brewin, C. R. *Posttraumatic Stress Disorder: Malady or Myth?* New Haven: Yale University Press, 2003.

Church, J. E. *Every Man a Bible Student.* Exeter: Paternoster Press Ltd, 1938/1976.

Colliander, T. "On the Insufficiency of Human Strength." In *Way of the Ascetics: The Ancient Tradition of Discipline and Inner Growth*, edited by T. Colliander, translated by K. Ferre. New York: St. Vladimirs Press, 1985.

Dallaire, R. *Shake Hands with the Devil: The Failure of Humanity in Rwanda.* London: Arrow Books, 2004.

———. "Trial, the Struggle." In *Seeking the Sacred: Leading a Spiritual Life in a Secular World*, edited by M. Joseph, 43–62. Ontario: ECW Press, 2006.

Diamond, J. *Life Energy: Using the Meridians to Unlock the Hidden Power of Your Emotions.* St. Paul, MN: Paragon House, 1985/1990.

———. *The Third Chimpanzee: The Evolution and Future of the Human Animal.* London: Harper Perennial, 1992.

Figley, C. R. "Compassion Fatigue as a Secondary Traumatic Stress Disorder: An Overview." In *Compassion Fatigue: Coping With Secondary Traumatic Stress Disorder in Those Who Treat the Traumatized*, edited by C. R. Figley, 1–20. Florence, KY: Brunner Mazel, 1995.

Frey, R. *The Genocidal Temptation: Auschwitz, Hiroshima, Rwanda, and Beyond.* Lanham, Maryland: University Press of America, 2004.

Gatwa, T. *The Churches and Ethnic Ideology in the Rwandan Crises 1900–1994*. Bletchley, Milton Keynes: Regnum Books, 2005.

Giradet, E. *Investing in Peace: Interpeace Annual Report 2005*. Geneva: Interpeace, 2006.

Goff, B. S. N. and K. L. Schwedrdtfeger. "The Systemic Impact of Traumatized Children." In *Handbook of Stress, Trauma and the Family*, edited by D. R. Catherall, 179–202. Hove: Brunner-Routledge, 2004.

Gold, S. N. "The Contextual Treatment Model." In *Handbook of Stress, Trauma and the Family* edited by D. R. Catherall, 347–366. New York: Brunner Routledge, 2004.

Goleman, D. *Social Intelligence: The New Science of Human Relationship*. London: Hutchinson, 2006.

Gourevitch, P. *We Wish to Inform You that Tomorrow We Will Be Killed with Our Families*. New York: Picador, 1998.

Green, E. M. B. *The Meaning of Salvation*. London: Hodder & Stoughton, 1965.

Guillebaud, M. *Rwanda: The Land God Forgot? Revival, Genocide, and Hope*. Mill Hill, London: Monarch Books, 2002.

Harris, C. J. "Sensory-Based Therapy for Crisis Counsellors." In *Compassion Fatigue: Coping with Secondary Traumatic Stress Disorder in Those Who Treat the Traumatized*, edited by C. R. Figley, 101–114. Florence, KY: Brunner Mazel, 1995.

Hegeman, E. and A. Wohl. "Management of Trauma-Related Affect, Defences and Dissociative States." In *Group Psychotherapy for Psychological Trauma*, edited by R. H. Klein and V. L. Schermer, 64–88. London: Guilford Press, 2000.

Heider, G. C. "Molech." In *The Dictionary of Deities and Demons in the Bible*, edited by K. V. D. Toorn, et al. Leiden: Brill, 1995.

Henderson, I. "Self-Love." In *The Westminster Dictionary of Christian Ethics*, edited by J. F. Childress and J. MacQuarrie. Philadelphia: Westminster Press, 1986.

Herman, J. L. *Trauma and Recovery*. London: Pandora, 1997.

Hession, R. *Calvary Road*. Alresford, Hants: CLC, 1950/1988.

Hicks, P. *The Message of Evil and Suffering*. Nottingham: IVP, 2006.

Hildebrandt, J. *History of the Church in Africa: A Survey*. Achimota, Ghana: African Christian Press, 1981.

Hirschhorn, L. "The Modern Project and the Feminisation of Men." In *Organisations, Anxieties, and Defences: Toward a Psychoanalytic Social Psychology*, edited by R. D. Hinshelwood and M. Chiesa, 35–64. London: Whurr Publishers, 2002.

Holmes, P. R. *Becoming More Human: Exploring the Interface of Spirituality, Discipleship and Therapeutic Faith Community*. Bletchley, Milton Keynes: Paternoster, 2005.

Holmes, P. R. and S. B. Williams. *Becoming More Like Christ: Introducing a Biblical Contemporary Journey*. Milton Keynes: Paternoster, 2007.

———. *Church as a Safe Place: A Handbook Confronting, Resolving and Minimising Abuse in the Church*. Bletchley: Authentic, 2007.

Holmes, T. "The Acceleration of Global Violence." <http://www.simplyted.blogspot.com/2005/07/acceleration-of-global-violence.html>.

Joseph, M. *Seeking the Sacred: Leading a Spiritual Life in a Secular World*. Ontario: ECW Press, 2006.

Kaplan, T. "Psychological Responses to Interpersonal Violence: Children." In *Psychological Trauma: A Developmental Approach*, edited by D. Black, et al., 184–198. London: Gaskell, 1997.

Kauffman, R. A. "Suffering God," *Christianity Today*. (2007): 71.

Kelly, H. A. *Satan: A Biography*. Cambridge: Cambridge University Press, 2006.

Klein, R. H. and V. L. Schermer. *Group Psychotherapy for Psychological Trauma*. London: Guilford Press, 2000.

Kolini, E., M. *Biblical Ecclesiology*. Alexandria: Virginia Seminary, 1997.

Kritzinger, J. J. *The Rwandan Tragedy as a Public Indictment Against Christian Mission*. Missionalia, 2007.

Krug, E. G., et al. *World Report on Violence and Health*. Geneva: World Health Organization, 2002.

Llibagiza, I. *Left to Tell: Discovering God Amidst the Rwandan Holocaust*. London: Hay House, 2006.

Ludwig, E. *The Nile: The Life Story of a River*. George Allen and Unwin Ltd, 1940.

Mamdani, M. *When Victims Become Killers: Colonialism, Nativism, and the Genocide in Rwanda*. Kampala & Dar es Salaam: Fountain, 2001.

Martin, D. V. *Adventure in Psychiatry: Social Change in a Mental Hospital*. London: Bruno Cassirer Publications, 1962.

Martin, P. *The Sickening Mind: Brain, Behaviour, Immunity Disease*. London: Flamingo, 1998.

Matsakis, A. "Trauma and Its Impact on Families." In *Handbook of Stress, Trauma and the Family*, edited by D. R. Catherall, 15–32. New York: Brunner Routledge, 2004.

Meeks, W. A. *The Origins of Christian Morality: The First Two Centuries*. New Haven: Yale University Press, 1993.

Melvern, L. R. *A People Betrayed: The Role of the West in Rwanda's Genocide*. London: Zed Books, 2000.

Meredith, M. *The State of Africa: A History of Fifty Years of Independence*. London: Free Press, 2005.

Mezey, G. "Psychological Responses to Interpersonal Violence: Adults." In *Psychological Trauma: A Developmental Approach*, edited by D. Black, et al, 176–183. London: Gaskell, 1997.

Minneart, P. S. M. A. *Premier Voyage de Mgr Hirth au Rwanda: Novembre 1899– Février 1900. Contribution à l'étude de la Fondation de l'Eglise Catholique au Rwanda.* Kigali: 2006.

Murekezi, A. A. "Don't Patronize or Belittle Rwandan Christians Committed to Progress." *Christianity Today.* <http://www.christianitytoday.com/ct/2006/004/19.98.html>.

National Institute for Clinical Excellence. *Post-Traumatic Stress Disorder: The Management of PTSD in Adults and Children in Primary and Secondary Care.* Gaskell & British Psychological Society, 2005.

Newbury, C. *The Cohesion of Oppression: Clientship and Ethnicity in Rwanda 1860–1960.* New York: Columbia University Press, 1988.

O'Mathuna, D. P. "Human Dignity in the Nazi Era: Implications for Contemporary Bioethics." *BMC Medicine.* <http://www.biomedcentral.com/1472-6939/7/2>.

Ogungbile, D. "Water Symbolism in African Culture and Afro Christian Churches." *Journal of Religious Thought* 53/54 (1997): 21–38.

Palachy, A. W. "Group Psychotherapy for Victims of Political Torture and Other Forms of Severe Ethnic Persecution." In *Group Psychotherapy for Psychological Trauma*, edited by R. H. Klein and V. L. Schermer, 265–297. London: Guilford Press, 2000.

Pearlman, L. A. and K. W. Saakvitne. "Treating Therapists with Vicarious Traumatization and Secondary Traumatic Stress Disorder." In *Compassion Fatigue: Coping with Secondary Traumatic Stress Disorder in Those Who Treat the Traumatized*, edited by C. R. Figley, 150–177. Florence, KY: Brunner Mazel, 1995.

Peter, C. M. and E. Kibalama, eds. *Civil Society and the Struggle for a Better Rwanda: A Report of the Fact-Finding Mission to Rwanda Organized Under the Auspices of Kituo Cha Katiba.* Kampala: Fountain Publishers, 2006.

Pownall, K. "Uganda's Daily Rate of Violent Death Is Three Times Iraq's, Says Report." *Independent.* London, March 30, 2006.

Prins, F. E. "Praise to the Bushmen Ancestors of the Water." In *Miscast: Negotiating the Presence of the Bushmen*, edited by P. Skotnes. Cape Town University Press, 1996.

Prunier, G. *The Rwanda Crisis: History of a Genocide.* New York: Columbia University Press, 1995.

Reader, J. *Africa: A Biography of the Continent.* London: Penguin, 1998.

Roegiere, P. *La Belgique: Le Roman d'un Pays.* Bruxelles: Gallimard Publishers, 2005.

Rowland-Klein, D. "The Transmission of Trauma Across Generations: Identification with Parental Trauma in Children of the Holocaust Survivors." In *Handbook of Stress, Trauma and the Family*, edited by D. R. Catherall, 117–138. New York: Brunner Routledge, 2004.

Royal College of Psychiatrists. *Post-Traumatic Stress Disorder: The Management of PTSD in Adults and Children in Primary and Secondary Care.* London: Gaskell, 2005.

Rummel, R. J. *Death by Government.* Piscataway, N. J.: Transaction Publishers, 1997.

Salzman, T. "Catholics & Colonialism: The Church's Failure in Rwanda." *High Beam Encyclopedia,* 1997. <Access http://www.encyclopedia.com/1G1-19962921.html>.

Sarfari, C. P. "Challenge to Reconciliation in Rwanda Following the 1994 Genocide: Theological Perspectives." <http://www.theo.kuleaven.be/page/doctoraltheses/107/>.

Shadle, B. "Patronage, Millenialism and the Serpent God Mumbo in South-West Kenya." *Africa* 72 (2002): 29–54.

Stanton, G. H. *Eight Stages of Genocide.* Washington: Department of State, 1998.

Tuhabonye, G. and G. Brozek. *A Genocide Survivor's Story of Escape, Faith and Forgiveness.* London: Harper Collins, 2006.

Vasina, J. *Antecedents to Modern Rwanda: The Nyiginya Kingdom.* Madison: University of Wisconsin Press, 2004.

Wikipedia. "Genocide." <http://en.wikipedia.org/wiki/Genocide>.

Wright, N. G. *A Theology of the Dark Side: Putting the Power of Evil in Its Place.* Carlisle: Paternoster Press, 2003.